Edward Adolphus Seymour Somerset, Edward Adolphus Seymour Somerset

Monarchy and Democracy

Phases of Modern Politics

Edward Adolphus Seymour Somerset, Edward Adolphus Seymour Somerset

Monarchy and Democracy
Phases of Modern Politics

ISBN/EAN: 9783743409736

Manufactured in Europe, USA, Canada, Australia, Japa

Cover: Foto ©Suzi / pixelio.de

Manufactured and distributed by brebook publishing software (www.brebook.com)

Edward Adolphus Seymour Somerset, Edward Adolphus Seymour Somerset

Monarchy and Democracy

MONARCHY AND DEMOCRACY

PHASES

OF

MODERN POLITICS

BY

THE DUKE OF SOMERSET, K.G.

In vetere novum latet ;
In novo vetus patet.

London
JAMES BAIN 1 HAYMARKET
1889

LONDON :

G. NORMAN AND SON, PRINTERS, 29, MAIDEN LANE,
COVENT GARDEN.

PREFACE.

AN endeavour is made in the following short and fragmentary chapters to trace the growth of modern political opinions. For this purpose the doctrines propounded by distinguished French, English, and American writers are cited, the value of their doctrines tested by later experience, and their predictions compared with subsequent events.

Our present form of government is a fusion of Monarchy and Democracy; in which fusion during the last fifty years Democracy has been continually advancing. Whether this movement indicates the progressive improvement of the constitution, or its deterioration and decay, is a question on which politicians will differ.

"To secure the advantages of government with the least possible inconvenience to the governed," is not a bad criterion of Statesmanship, but it is not the system which prevails in the present day. There is an incessant interference with the governed; and the legislation of every recurring session imposes some new restriction on human freedom. This constitutes only one of the problems submitted for consideration in the following pages, but it involves a principle which should be closely watched.

> "Est il donc, entre nous, rien de plus despotique
> Que l'esprit d'un état qui passe en république."

CONTENTS.

CHAP.   PAGE

   I. OF CONSTITUTIONAL SOVEREIGNTY .   .   1

  II. DAVID HUME ON OUR MIXED CONSTITUTION 26

 III. MODERN DEMOCRACY   34

  IV. THE THEORY OF JAMES MILL—POLITICAL
        SCIENCE BASED ON SELFISHNESS   . 52

   V. LORD MACAULAY'S THEORY—THE SCIENCE
        OF POLITICS FOUNDED ON INDUCTION 59

  VI. THE GREAT REPUBLIC   65

 VII. THE WORKING OF REPRESENTATIVE IN-
        STITUTIONS   85

VIII. THE POLITICS OF THE PROLETARIAT   . 92

  IX. PUBLIC SPEAKING AT PARTY GATHERINGS 95

   X. EDUCATION THE SAFEGUARD OF SOCIETY . 102

  XI. THE FUNCTIONS OF THE GOVERNMENT . 114

  XII. OF LIBERTY   124

 XIII. OF ARISTOCRACY   136

 XIV. ENVY THE ANIMATING SPIRIT OF DEMOCRACY 154

  XV. THE MINISTERS OF A CONSTITUTIONAL KING 158

 XVI. OF PROGRESS   177

CHAPTER I.

OF CONSTITUTIONAL SOVEREIGNTY.

THE vague rumours which have been lately buzzed about in reference to some undue exercise of the royal prerogative, and to the introduction of personal government in the management of foreign affairs, naturally direct attention to the present position in this country of a constitutional sovereign.

Constitutional kingship, or, as it was commonly called, limited monarchy, is a contrivance of modern growth, although the rudiments of the system may be traced in the early history of many European states.

What should be the limits of a limited monarchy, is a question on which opposite opinions have been pronounced with some bitterness.

I

These opinions are founded on two different theories which can never be completely reconciled.

The regal government in European countries was not originally established on any uniform or systematic plan. It seems to have been the result of two antagonistic principles ; one derived from the Roman law, which invested the sovereign with the whole power of the state; the other transmitted from the usages of northern nations, who regarded their king as their leader in time of war, and as the president of the assembled freemen in time of peace.

The maxims of the lawyers and the precepts of the clergy supported the absolute authority of the sovereign against the unwritten usages and traditions of the freemen ; but as the freemen were armed, they were able to resist any encroachment of the regal power by which they felt themselves aggrieved.

At a later period these two antagonistic

principles, under the two heads of prerogative and privilege, caused a conflict which occupies a large space in English history.   Here it may suffice to observe, that the contention was finally closed in the year 1688 by a convenient but somewhat illogical compromise.

The accession of the Hanoverian dynasty facilitated a more formal settlement of this anomalous system; which may be thus stated.

The constitutional king retains the transcen-\ dent attributes of sovereignty.   He represents in his person the whole power and authority of the state.   He is acknowledged as reigning by the grace of God, and *Dei gratiâ* is stamped on his coins.   His person is sacred.   He can do no wrong, and while he is not amenable to any earthly tribunal, his subjects are bound to obey his commands.

On the other hand, the Constitution reminds the king that he reigns by the Act of Settlement.   He finds, moreover, that he can perform no act of sovereignty except through the

1 *

agency of a minister, who is presumed to have advised the act, and is held responsible for it. The minister, again, cannot plead as a justification of his conduct, that he acted under the direct command of the king; such a plea would be an aggravation of the offence, as it would bring obloquy on his royal master.

To this extent the authority of the sovereign is restricted by the Constitution, and even where the law sanctions the royal power, it is now extinguished by disuse. The sovereign has the power of veto on any bill which has passed through both Houses of Parliament, but prescriptive custom now forbids him to impose this veto.

Thus the plenitude of kingly power, although nominally supreme, is limited in its exercise, and the result is an incongruous mixture, which admits of different interpretations according to the opinions entertained by high legal authorities, learned historians, and distinguished statesmen.

On this important constitutional matter it will not be uninstructive to recall the written opinion of a Lord Chancellor, who exercised great influence at a momentous crisis of our national affairs.

A CONSTITUTIONAL SOVEREIGN.

The late Lord Brougham, in his Sketch of George III, discusses the position of a constitutional sovereign.

" The question is, Does the king of this country hold a real or only a nominal office ? Is he merely a form, or is he a substantive power in our mixed and balanced Constitution ? Some maintain, nay, it is a prevailing opinion among certain authorities of no mean rank, that the sovereign, having chosen his ministers, assigns over to them the whole executive power. They treat him as a kind of trustee for a temporary use, to preserve, as it were, some contingent estate ; or a provisional assignee, to hold the property of an insolvent for a day, and then divest himself of the estate by assigning it over. They regard the only power really vested in the Crown to be the choice of ministers, and even the exercise of this to be controlled by the Parliament. They reduce the king more completely to the condition of a state pageant or state cipher than one of Abbé Sieyes's Constitutions did, when he proposed to have a Grand Functionary with no power except to give away offices; upon which Napoleon, then First Consul, to whom the proposition was tendered, asked if it well became him to be a ' cochon à l'engrais à la somme de trois millions par an ?'

" The English animal, according to the Whig doctrine, much more nearly answers this somewhat coarse description ; for the Abbé's plan was to give his royal beast a substantial voice in the distribution of all patronage ; while our lion is only to have the sad prerogative of naming whomsoever the Parliament chooses, and eating his own mess in quiet.

" Now (Lord Brougham continues) with all the disposition in the world to desire that royal prerogative should be restricted, and the will of the nation govern the national affairs, we cannot comprehend this theory of a monarchy. It assigns to the Crown either far too much revenue, or far too little power. To pay a million a-year, or more, for a name, seems absurdly extravagant. To affect living under a kingly government, and yet suffer no kind of kingly power, seems extravagantly absurd. Surely the meaning of having a sovereign is, that his voice should be heard and his influence felt in the administration of public affairs. The different orders of the state have a right to look towards that high quarter, all in their turn, for support when their rights are invaded by one another's encroachments, or to claim the royal umpirage when their mutual conflicts cannot be settled by mutual concessions ; and unless the whole notion of a mixed monarchy and a balance of three powers is a mere fiction and a dream, the royal portion of the composition must be allowed to have some power, to produce some effect upon the quality of the whole."

Such was the opinion of Lord Brougham when as an author he treated of the power of a constitutional king. When, however, Lord Brougham was Lord Chancellor, his conduct was hardly in accordance with this deliberately written opinion; for he did not yield to his sovereign that kingly power which should, he said, be associated with kingly government.

William IV ascended the throne in the year 1830. at the age of sixty-five. Within a few weeks of his accession a revolution occurred in France, which disturbed Continental states, and excited a general commotion in this country. The king desired to retain the administration of which the Duke of Welling-ton was the head, and this ministry, as may be seen in the published correspondence of the Duke, enjoyed the complete confidence of the sovereign. The Duke's foreign policy was not popular, and his avowed determination to resist all reform of the representation rendered his home policy unacceptable to the country. The result of the general election made a change of ministers inevitable, and the new ministers were pledged to Parliamentary reform. William, although disinclined to any great constitutional change, desired honestly to fulfil the duties of his station, to act as umpire between the two parties struggling for power, and to preserve that traditional balance of King, Lords, and Commons, which he venerated as the sacred palladium of the British Constitution.

William IV believed that his royal prerogative entitled him to decide on the appointment of his ministers, on the dissolution of Parliament, and on the creation of peers.

Desiring to keep strictly within the lines of the Constitution, he gave a frank support to his new ministers. Although seriously alarmed by the comprehensive measure of Parliamentary reform which was proposed to him, the King, after much correspondence with Earl Grey, his Prime Minister, and many futile endeavours to qualify the scheme, reluctantly yielded to the opinion of the Cabinet, and allowed his ministers to introduce their Reform Bill.

In making this concession William accompanied it with a reservation, which he deemed to be his legitimate prerogative. This he was careful to state in a letter of the 21st March, 1831, to Earl Grey in these words : " the King considered a dissolution in the existing state of the country to be fraught with danger, and he deemed it his duty to forewarn the Cabinet that his objection to a dissolution of Parliament was final and conclusive." In order that there might be no misconception of his opinion on this subject, he repeated it emphatically as " his firm unalterable decision."

Nevertheless on the 21st April, within a month of this solemn announcement, the helpless

King was compelled, under the pressure of his ministers (Lord Brougham being especially urgent), to come himself to the House of Lords, and announce the prorogation with a view to the immediate dissolution of Parliament.

This would appear to have been a case where, as Lord Brougham writes, the conflict of parties could not be settled by mutual concessions, and where consequently the royal umpire might advantageously have interfered to allay the violence of factions.

So far, however, from allowing the King to exert his influence for this purpose, the ministers, amongst whom Lord Brougham was most energetic, terrified the sovereign with predictions of an overwhelming disaster, and forced him to become the leader of a party, instead of acting as the supreme arbiter of the state.

Thus William found himself constrained to exercise two of his prerogatives, contrary to his own judgment, in submissive obedience to his ministers. He had still one prerogative left, namely, the power of creating peers. Here again he would have been compelled to exercise his kingly power at the bidding of the Cabinet, if the peers had not saved the sovereign from this further humiliation by abdicating their lawful functions.

Throughout these proceedings William IV was reduced to a "state pageant" or "ornamental cipher." The royal voice was indeed heard, and the royal influence felt, but in direct contradiction to the royal will. This is now clearly manifested by the published correspondence of Earl Grey, who was then Prime Minister.

Thus it is evident that Lord Brougham, although he repudiated and decried what he called the Whig doctrine, in his book, yet adopted and enforced it with the utmost rigour in his official capacity.

On this occasion the sovereign was set aside, and he showed how deeply he resented this treatment by taking the first opportunity of dismissing these domineering ministers. Lord Spencer's death necessitated some change in the public departments, but the King determined to change the ministry, and accordingly appointed Sir Robert Peel (who was then in Italy) to form another administration.

By this hasty and injudicious use of the prerogative, the King exposed his new minister to a defeat, and subjected himself to a further humiliation.

It will be probably admitted that King William would better have consulted his own happiness and royal dignity, if, instead of persisting in a lengthened and abortive correspondence with his Prime Minister, Earl Grey, he had abstained from expressing any political opinion, and had limited his functions to the formal duties inseparable from a constitutional monarchy.

The period of William's accession may however be designated as an exceptional era in our constitutional history. The ministers of that day, in order to succeed in carrying a measure of Parliamentary reform, stirred the whole country into a phrenzy of excitement ; they threatened and overpowered the King, whilst they promised benefits to the working class which were not fulfilled.

The demand for a further reform, and for, what was then called, the People's Charter, originated from popular disappointment at the result of a measure which conferred no immediate benefit on the working men.

The revolutionary violence of the reform crisis tended to lower the position of the sovereign, and to disparage his influence in the administration of public affairs. It is necessary therefore to take a wider view of the kingly power throughout several reigns.

Our political experience on this subject is unfortunately limited.

The constitutional machinery can hardly be said to have been in working order during the two reigns which immediately followed the revolution of 1688, and it worked at great disadvantage under the succeeding kings.

George I having passed the middle age of life before he ascended the throne, being equally ignorant of the language and of the feelings of his British subjects, naturally entrusted the affairs of this kingdon to the statesmen and to the political party to whom he owed the crown.

He was proud of being a king, but German politics and the interests of Hanover occupied his chief attention. Nevertheless, he performed the duties of his high station sufficiently well under the guidance of his ministers.

His reign did not, however, enhance the authority or the dignity of the Crown.

George II also discharged the duties of his position with fairness and judgment, when the more attractive interests of his German electorate did not interfere with the policy submitted for his approval.

These two kings in private life were not

more refined than their subjects. They had no deep sense of religion, and little regard for propriety of conduct. It must, however, be admitted that during these two reigns this country advanced in wealth and general prosperity more rapidly than at any former period. Hallam, an impartial historian, even ventured to assert : " The reign of George II might not disadvantageously be compared for the real happiness of the people with that more brilliant but uncertain and oscillatory condition which has since ensued."

The attachment of these kings to their German possessions proved to be detrimental to British interests ; and the personal influence of the sovereign in the conduct of foreign affairs entangled the English Government in Continental disputes and alliances, which rendered the King unpopular, and brought discredit on the King's ministers.

George III differed from his predecessors in determining to be a governing king.   His

mother had imbued his youthful mind with
this notion, but did not confer upon him an
education qualifying him for this task. He
was attentive to public business, studious of
official details, resolute in maintaining the
prerogative, and jealous of any encroachment
on, what he believed to be, the legitimate
rights of the Crown. The strict regularity
of his private life contrasted favourably with
the habits of his predecessors, and by com-
manding universal respect, strengthened his
royal authority.

In his attempt to guide the course of public
affairs he conscientiously believed that he was
only vindicating his due share of political
power. Thus the King wrote to Mr. Pitt:
" There are two prerogatives which I cannot
allow to be infringed—namely, the power of
negativing bills which have passed both
Houses of Parliament, and that of naming the
ministers to be employed; without these two
powers I can no longer be of utility to this

2

country, nor can with honour continue in this island."

It is now manifest that George III never understood the position of a constitutional sovereign ; he had however acuteness enough to perceive that supreme authority could only be attained by acquiring a predominant influence in the House of Commons. With this view, therefore, according to the language of Burke, " the King abandoned the old-fashioned fortress of prerogative, and made a lodgment in the stronghold of Parliament itself."

The result was disastrous both at home and abroad. The House of Commons, being notoriously influenced by the King, was distrusted by the people, and even the Corporation of London was alienated from its traditional loyalty to the House of Hanover. George III, moreover, in the anxiety of these incessant struggles with his ministers and his Parliament, deranged the balance of a mind verging on insanity, and then blamed his ministers for discomposing his shattered intellect.

The prolongation of the war with North America, and the obstinate refusal to consider a timely adjustment of the Roman Catholic claims, need only be mentioned to recall the serious and enduring mischief occasioned by the conscientious but injudicious policy of this unfortunate sovereign.

It would, in truth, have been better both for the King himself and for the country, if George III had imitated his immediate predecessors, and had relinquished the attempt to guide the policy of the state.

The interference of George IV in public affairs was mainly directed to two objects : the divorce of his wife, and the exclusion of the Roman Catholics from Parliament. In both these objects he was defeated, after having sullied his personal honour weakened the authority of his government,

2 *

and even endangered the tranquillity of the realm.

The history of the five reigns here shortly noticed, which however occupied a period of one hundred and twenty years, would lead to the conclusion that a constitutional sovereign will act wisely in restricting himself to his formal functions, and leaving to his ministers the trouble and odium of state affairs.

If this were the true theory of the British Constitution, it would be the wisest course for the king not to harass himself with the study of political affairs either domestic or foreign. Since he is not responsible, and cannot control hem, he should rest satisfied with the dignified splendour of his station, and amuse his leisure with the patronage of the fine arts, or with public ceremonies, where the gracious condescension of a king will always gain popular applause.

The qualities desirable in such a king would be of a neutral type. He might indeed with advantage possess what Shakespeare calls

"the King-becoming graces
As justice, verity, temperance, stableness,"

but vigorous intellectual faculties, earnest convictions, energy of character, warmth of feeling, and other endowments, which in private life attract affection and respect, would be misplaced and probably be mischievous in a constitutional king. Hallam observes, "A king possessed of ambitious views and gifted with great abilities might endanger the balance of the Constitution."

Even in his religious belief indifference will be preferable to zeal, for kings too often display their faith by persecuting or vexing some of their subjects. An active-minded king would assuredly form political opinions, and these may mar the equable temperament with which he should regard rival statesmen.

Personal attachments and aversions will interfere with the appointment of public

functionaries, and royal favourites are uni-
versally detested. George II objected to
Chatham, whom he called a trumpet of
sedition. George III declared he never would
accept Charles Fox as a minister. George IV
said he had made a vow to himself, which
as a gentleman he could not break, never to
admit Canning into the Cabinet.

In all these cases the king eventually
yielded; but not until much personal bitterness
had been created, and the national interests
had suffered from the private feelings or
political predilections of the sovereign.

A constitutional king must be prepared to
accept as his ministers men whom he distrusts,
and to ratify with his royal sanction measures
which he disapproves. From his elevated
station he must often see contending politicians
engaged in a selfish struggle for office, and
hazarding the permanent interest of the realm
for the sake of a party triumph.

Walter Bagehot, in his treatise on the

British Constitution, asserted, "The sovereign
has three rights : the right to be consulted, the
right to encourage, the right to warn, and a
king of great sense and sagacity should want
no others." ^

With all these rights a king may find
himself helpless in restraining a ministry, who
appeal to the passions, and gain the support, of
the most numerous and ignorant class of the
electors.

According to the theory of the British
Constitution, the ministers are responsible for
every act of the executive government, while
the sovereign is exempt from all responsibility.
A king who reflects upon his position will
perceive that this constitutional theory is
intrinsically false.

The ministers, after mismanaging the affairs
and diminishing the resources of the state, may
incur a Parliamentary defeat, and retire from
office. They immediately occupy the benches
of opposition, or sink into the insignificance of

private life.   The sovereign, however, remains, and he, or his successors in after years, must pay the penalty for an incapable or dishonest administration.

The Crown, although limited in power, is unlimited in its ultimate responsibility.

It is not, therefore, unreasonable in the sovereign to be an anxious politician. He cannot see with indifference a course of policy pursued which, while it strengthens a political party, may seriously imperil the permanent interests of state or impair the legitimate authority of the Crown.

He must often feel that his ministers, although nominally the servants of the sovereign, are under another allegiance, and with the growth of democracy the influence of this allegiance may preponderate even to the detriment of the monarchy.

The system of constitutional government established by the Revolution of 1688 required for its successful working a wise moderation on the part of the sovereign, and a considerate forbearance on the part of the representatives of the people.

This anomalous form of government had from the date of its birth many inherent difficulties, and those difficulties were often surmounted by expedients, which tarnished the honour of politicians, and tainted the atmosphere of public life.

David Hume, in his Political Essays, openly avowed an opinion that corruption in some form was a necessity as a counterpoise to the overwhelming power of the House of Commons.

CHAPTER II.

DAVID HUME ON OUR MIXED CONSTITUTION.

HUME, in one of his Political Essays, discusses the nature of our mixed Constitution, and the distribution of political power. "How much," he says, "it would have surprised such a genius as Cicero or Tacitus to have been told that in a future age there would arise a very regular system of mixed government, where the authority was so distributed that one rank, whenever it pleased, might swallow up all the rest, and engross the whole power of the Constitution. Such a government, they would say, will not be a mixed government. For so great is the natural ambition of men, that they are never satisfied with power, and if one order of men by pursuing its own interest, can usurp upon every other order, it will certainly do so, and render itself, as far as possible, absolute and uncontrollable.

" By the British Constitution the power allotted to the House of Commons is so great that it absolutely commands all the other parts of the government. How, then," Hume asks, " shall we solve this paradox ? By what means is the House of Commons confined within its proper limits, since, from our Constitution, it must necessarily have as much power as it demands, and can only be confined by itself ?"

Hume's solution of this paradox is stated in the following words :—

" The patronage of the Crown and the many offices at its disposal will, when assisted by the honest and disinterested part of the House, command the resolutions of the whole body, so far at least as to preserve the ancient Constitution from danger."

" We may," Hume observes, " call this by the invidious appellations of corruption and dependence, but some degree and some kind of it are inseparable from the very nature of the Constitution, and necessary to the preservation of our mixed government."

On all political affairs experience is the safest guide. Hume wrote these pages about the year 1740, and as the Constitution of which he speaks can hardly be said to have existed before the year 1688, he necessarily founded his opinion on the history of fifty years. This was a period during which gross corruption had prevailed. Patronage exercised great influence in England, and was omnipotent in Scotland, The union with Scotland had not been accomplished without profuse pecuniary inducements. Hume, moreover, had grown up to manhood, and was then writing during the administration of Sir Robert Walpole, when the management of the House of Commons was first reduced to a system.

The Minister purchased the votes of members, who with unblushing effrontery asked for payment in return for their support of the Government. So long as the Minister could buy a sufficient number of members, it was unnecessary to bribe the constituencies, or to purchase seats in Parliament.

THE PURCHASE OF SEATS.

It is said that the purchase of seats in the House of Commons was introduced by the mercantile and moneyed men, who found themselves excluded from Parliament by the country gentlemen and land owners. The necessity of possessing land as a qualification for Parliament was a condition imposed for the purpose of excluding these moneyed men.

The practice of purchasing seats, although it corrupted the electors, brought into the House of Commons many useful members. Indeed, a wealthy man, who had purchased his seat, could exercise an independent judgment on public affairs, without the risk which at present attaches to freedom of opinion.

Many a candidate undoubtedly bought a seat or bribed a constituency as a profitable speculation, and having first paid the electors, afterwards sold himself to the Government. " Emerat ille prius, vendere jure potest."

With the increase of national wealth, electoral corruption became almost universal. In the reign of George III, the King entered the market with great spirit, the Ministry and the Opposition competed for seats, and boroughs were openly sold by auction.

Nevertheless through all this mass of venality and vice, public opinion exercised considerable power, and the British Constitution with all its defects was probably the best form of government which the world had as yet seen.

The securities, which Hume deemed indispensable for the preservation of our mixed Constitution, have been seriously impaired. The ministers can no longer dispose of seats in the House of Commons ; and although they can still bestow on their supporters lucrative appointments and honours, yet their control over the representatives of the people is so far diminished, that the Constitution described by Hume has ceased to exist.

It must not be assumed that the Parliamentary reform of 1832 put an end to corruption. On the contrary, during the twenty years which followed, pecuniary corruption in the large towns as well as in the small boroughs was probably more general than in any former time. The close boroughs and the old monopoly of representation were, for the most part, extinguished ; but a free-trade in corruption succeeded, as might easily be proved by a reference to the election committees of that period.

Stringent laws gradually repressed this form of corruption, and a further extension of the franchise has given an additional impulse to the democratic element in our mixed Constitution.

The problem therefore now presents itself,
Will the reasoning which Hume ascribed to
Cicero and Tacitus prove correct? Will the
House of Commons engross the whole power
of the state, and render itself absolute and
uncontrollable?

Political predictions are usually falsified by
subsequent events, and probably the British
Constitution may survive the loss of the
securities which David Hume considered to
be indispensable for its existence.

Since the time when Hume wrote these
essays more than a century has elapsed, and
other forces have been brought into operation.
The House of Commons has gained power, but
its reputation has diminished. The Crown,
although apparently shorn of its ancient
authority, has acquired greater influence in
the conduct of public affairs.

The ministers of the sovereign, holding
office by an uncertain and precarious tenure,
have less power than at any former period of

English history. The executive government, feeble at home and unable to pass any measure except by means of some popular clamour, is paralyzed in its foreign policy.

Democracy, so far as limited experience enables us to form an opinion, is a system of government ill-fitted for the management of distant dependencies, and for negociations with foreign states.

CHAPTER III.

MODERN DEMOCRACY.

AMID the commotions of the seventeenth century there arose a party called Independents, or root-and-branch men, who were desirous to abolish monarchy and to establish a republican form of government.

Oliver Cromwell was the soul of that party; his genius raised it to power, his ambition brought it into discredit, and at his death it ceased to have any political influence. The Independents, indeed, survived as a religious sect, who cherished the memory of what they called "the good old cause," and were the ardent assertors of civil and religious liberty, which they held to be hardly reconcilable with regal government.

Meanwhile discussions upon the origin of

civil government, and upon the rights of kings and of subjects, occupied the attention of political writers. Sir Robert Filmer, by his attempt to vindicate the divine right of kings, excited a controversy leading to a directly opposite result, and induced many persons to read the heavy folio of Algernon Sidney, or to study the argumentative essay of Locke.

Questions respecting the origin of political societies, and the rights which man possesses by nature, may amuse the leisure of philosophical students, but become mischievous when appealed to for the guidance of men living under the artificial conditions of modern civilization.

POLITICAL RIGHT AND RIGHTS.

Few words in the political vocabulary have caused more confusion and disturbance than the word "right" in the singular and in the plural. The French equivalent "droit" has exercised an equally turbulent influence.

3 *

Political philosophers have not succeeded in affixing a precise meaning to this ambiguous term. Hobbes asserted as an absolute and fundamental truth : " There is nothing to which every man has not a right by nature." Here another doubtful word is joined to the word right, and it was assumed that right was derived from what was called nature. The Latin word " jus " conveys a more definite meaning than the word right, and when Roman lawyers employed the phrase " jus naturæ," they attempted to remedy the defects of existing laws by an appeal to the first principles of justice, which they assumed to be the ordinance of nature. This fiction, when applied by jurists to the interpretation of law, may have exercised a salutary influence, but when it was associated with political theories it tended to the confusion and disquietude of civilized society.

There is a certain order or regularity in the phenomena of the visible world, and this has been denominated law of nature. The phrase was not well chosen, as it assumed a similarity between the inflexible regularity of nature and the fluctuating codes of human legislation.

The most violent conflict which the word right has occasioned arose long since from the antagonism between the right of the sovereign and the rights of the subject. The right of the sovereign was glorified by flattery into divine right. The rights of the subject were magnified by fiction into the rights of man. These two delusions produced deplorable consequences, and have stained with blood the saddest pages of history.

England had its full share of these troubles; but fortunately the practical statesmen, to whom we owe our constitutional freedom, did not perplex themselves with theories of natural rights and laws of nature, but founding their claims on the Great Charter (which Hallam justly calls the keystone of English freedom) proceeded to assert in the Petition of Right, in

the Declaration of Rights, and in the Bill of
Rights, the demands which they held to be the
undoubted birthright and inheritance of the
people of England.

These demands were not, however, fully
conceded and confirmed, until a change of
dynasty had bound together the title of the
sovereign with the clearly defined rights of the
subject.

About the middle of the last century some
celebrated Frenchmen (the authors of an
Encyclopædia) and eloquent writers, amongst
whom Rousseau was pre-eminent, treated this
theory of natural right as the proper basis on
which all government should be founded.
They had no experience of public affairs, and
whenever they referred to history they selected
examples from Greek or Roman traditions.
They reasoned, however, less from history than
from what they assumed to be the natural
condition of man. They did not study this
condition ethnographically, but imagined a

primitive man, and ascribed to this ideal being the faculties and feelings of a Frenchman under the rule of Lewis XV.

Thus having observed that in England Parliamentary government afforded some security for liberty, they asserted without hesitation that to vote in a deliberative assembly was a natural right of all human beings.

Diderot extended this right to the whole animal creation. He wrote :—

" Si même les animaux pouvaient communiquer avec nous, et voter dans une assemblée générale, il faudrait les y appeler, et alors les questions de droit naturel ne se debattraient plus par devant l'humanité mais par devant l'animalité."

The French nation had been for so long a period excluded from all state affairs, and unaccustomed to political discussion, that they were bewildered and dazzled by what was presented to them as the elementary principles of human society. The government had been omnipotent, and consequently the people expected everything from it. Even the philosophic mind of Montesquieu ascribed to the state duties which no state could adequately perform. In the twenty-ninth chapter of the twenty-third book of " L'Esprit des Lois," he ventured to affirm :—

" L'état doit à tous les citoyens une subsistance assurée, la nourriture, un vêtement convenable, et un genre de vie qui ne soit point contraire à la santé."

This language from a man who had held a high magisterial position, and who was engaged in writing an elaborate work on Jurisprudence, seemed to justify the wildest demands of the revolutionary rabble. If such were the duties of the state, they were also the rights of the subject.

The dreams of the (so-called) Socialists could hardly picture a more fanciful commonwealth than Montesquieu would have established, if he could have enforced the principles which he thus inconsiderately avowed.

The democratic literature of France even coloured the language of English politicians in the early part of George III's reign. One example will suffice, and it shall be from a member of the House of Lords, and from a man whose legal knowledge raised him to the highest honours of his profession. In a speech of March, 1766, on the subject of American taxation, Lord Camden declared : " Taxation and representation are inseparably united ; God has joined them ; no British Parliament can separate them. This position I repeat, and will maintain it to my last hour; it is founded on the law of nature ; it is itself an eternal law of nature," &c., &c.

The peers of England were thus assured by a high legal authority that God Almighty had ordained taxation and representation, and joined them together. This, moreover, was solemnly proclaimed to be an eternal law of nature.

Is it surprising that the science of politics made little progress when statesmen, who were regarded as oracles of law, talked such extravagant nonsense ? Lord Camden might as reasonably have maintained that God Almighty had ordained vote by ballot.

Meanwhile the popular doctrine of natural rights crossed the Atlantic and found a congenial soil in North America, where the colonists had been recently provoked to revolt by the impolitic legislation of Great Britain. Jefferson and his colleagues, in the celebrated Declaration of Independence, did not base their claims on their English birthright and inheritance, but preferred to borrow from the political philosophy of the French people. In imitation of the French philosophers, the American Congress proclaimed the natural equality of men, and appealed to the inalienable rights with which, they said, God had endowed the whole human race.

As a war-cry, this language answered its

purpose; it rallied the colonists, and attracted the popular sympathy of Europe. The French king and queen, hoping to gain popularity by humiliating England, encouraged the revolt, not foreseeing the perils of the new principles which they patronized.

Soon, however, the democratic dogma, triumphant in America, was wafted back to Europe by the breath of a victorious people. Great Britain recovered from the shock, but the throne of the Bourbons was laid prostrate in the dust.

This appeal to natural right had some inconvenience even in America. In after years when the red Indian claimed his hunting-grounds, and the rights which God had given him, the glorious manifesto was repudiated. When the black African piteously asked for some portion of these rights, his petition was rejected with contempt. Even now the native of China will receive but a scant share of these inalienable rights.

In the year 1789, when the French Assembly
undertook to regenerate human society
throughout the world, they deemed it necessary to define the natural rights of man before
proceeding to discuss his civil rights. During
a period when lawless confusion prevailed,
when riotous and drunken mobs were murder-
ing and plundering in the provinces; the
orators of the Convention passed many weeks
in delivering elaborate essays on the natural
rights of man. " Fatras métaphysique,
bavardage assommant !" They were clever
logicians and subtle reasoners, but nevertheless
in their declamations they found themselves
confronted with this difficulty : If the natural
rights of man are inalienable and paramount
to all human enactments, how can any
assembly restrict these natural rights by
legislation ? Unless every living man and
woman in the country consent to such restriction, the law is an unjustifiable act of tyranny !
Consent to every law must be renewed by

every successive generation, otherwise the people are deprived of their natural rights. Here was an insuperable dilemma.

The only escape was, to leave the natural rights of man in abeyance, and to turn their attention to man's civil rights.

In the midst of a community maddened by famine, by the sight of surrounding destitution, and by a deep sense of injustice, it was found impossible to re-establish social order, until natural rights and civil rights perished simultaneously under the iron rule of the Empire.

The notion of man's natural rights spread, however, like an epidemic among the poorest class, who were dissatisfied with the hardships of life and with the unequal conditions of civilized society. Politicians in this country, who called themselves the friends of the people, helped to propagate the belief that the natural rights of man would form a secure basis for the reconstruction of society. Mackintosh, a man learned in history and in

law, ventured to assert that "the French people
had founded a Constitution on the immutable
basis of natural right and general happiness."
He furthermore predicted that "the French
nation instead of the glories of war, would now
seek a new splendour in cultivating the arts of
peace and extending the happiness of mankind."

Such was the vain hope of the "Vindiciæ
Gallicæ," published in the year 1791. A prediction refuted by twenty years of European
war.

What can be said for the science of politics
when its professors blunder so egregiously?

The violent feelings generated in this
country by the French Revolution clouded the
soberest intellects, and produced a delirium
incompatible with the examination of the
complex problems of human society.

Edmund Burke, in his "Reflections on the
French Revolution," had previously attempted
to correct popular errors on this equivocal

word "rights." He however avoided "natural rights," and confined his observations to civil rights. "If civil society be made for the advantage of man, all the advantages for which it is made become his right. It is an institution of beneficence acting by rule. Men have a right to live by that rule; they have a right to justice; they have a right to the fruits of their industry, and the means of making their industry fruitful. They have a right to the acquisitions of their parents, to the nourishment and improvement of their off-spring, to instruction in life, and to consolation in death.

"Whatever each man can do without trespassing upon others, he has a right to do for himself; and he has a right to a fair portion of all which society, with all its combinations of skill and force, can do in his favour. In this partnership all men have equal rights, but not to equal things. He that has but five shillings in the partnership, has as good a right to it, as he that has five hundred pounds has to his larger portion.

"I have in contemplation the civil social man and no other; and as to the share of power, authority, and direction which each individual ought to have in the management of the state, that I must deny to be amongst the direct original rights of man in civil society."

Burke's reasoning was somewhat confused, and open to the objections which Mackintosh, Thomas Paine, and other writers urged against it.

When Burke asserted "Civil society is an institution of beneficence," the answer was obvious; the institution may be so corrupt that its beneficence is nullified.

The condition of the civil social man (to use Burke's phrase) had in France become intolerable, and human nature revolted. It was a condition of which the Abbé Galiani truly observed: "Ad hæc tempora ventum est, ubi nec mala nec remedia pati possumus."

All this vague language about the natural rights or original rights of man will convince every thoughtful reader, that it is as difficult to analyze the elementary principles on which human society is founded, as it is to resolve into their primary ingredients the material objects of the visible world.

The root-and-branch men of the seventeenth century, the revolutionist of the eighteenth century, and the Radical in the early part of the nineteenth century, all aimed at some reconstruction of the whole social fabric.

Democracy was discredited in this country by the atrocities and follies of the French Government during, what was called, the Reign of Terror. So long, again, as the war with the first Napoleon occupied the mind of the nation, questions of internal government remained in abeyance, but on the restoration of peace, public opinion was directed to the reforms which had been advocated by statesmen in the previous century.

The cessation of war expenditure, combined·

with other causes, produced much distress among the labouring classes, and led to tumultuous meetings and riots. The Tory Government of that day, taking advantage of the general feeling against these rioters, denounced all reformers as revolutionists.

Thus many sober-minded men who were loyally attached to the British Constitution, but who held that our representative system required enlargement and amelioration, were induced to unite with more violent reformers. The country was gradually divided into two camps; the calm consideration of our representative institutions was rendered impossible, and a strong impulse was given to the party who were denominated Radicals.

THE GROWTH OF RADICALISM.

" Radice in Tartara tendit."—CANNING.

There were, soon after the peace of 1815, two classes of men who were called Radicals. One class consisted of indigent and ignorant men, whom noisy orators instigated to acts of

violence, which they themselves carefully es-
chewed ; the other class consisted of thoughtful
politicians, who discussed and expounded
theories of government. These men held
democracy to be the only rational system of
government, pretended to test every institution
by the principle of utility, despised all poetry as
silly exaggeration, and the fine arts as need-
less extravagance ; they disparaged the British
Constitution, which they regarded as an illogical
combination of conflicting authorities. Of this
class Jeremy Bentham was the oracle, and
James Mill the interpreter.

As a law reformer, Bentham has been de-
servedly praised, and his " Essay on Usury " is
admired for its argumentative vigour ; but on
questions of religion or of politics Bentham was
a destructive fanatic ; he could not write without bursting out in abusive epithets. Even in
his book on Fallacies, his political partiality
mars his judgment. According to his view,
ministers are the only disputants who employ
fallacious arguments.

4 *

CHAPTER IV.

THE THEORY OF JAMES MILL—POLITICAL SCIENCE BASED ON SELFISHNESS.

SOME fifty years have elapsed since James Mill published, in the " Encyclopædia Britannica," a treatise on " Government," which was presented to English readers as a scientific solution of the political problem. Mill undertook to demonstrate as a general proposition that democracy is the best form of government.

This treatise was regarded by the Radical reformers of that day as a masterpiece of political wisdom, and its leading principles were accepted as articles of faith in the democratic creed.

James Mill was a sincere Republican. He hated monarchy ; loathed all churches ; detested social rank; envied the rich, and desired to subvert the political and ecclesiastical institutions of the realm.

Mill asserted, as the basis of his political system, that the object of government should be to secure the greatest happiness of the greatest number.

The greatest number, that is the numerical majority of any political community, will always consist of the poorest class, the manual labourers. The whole object of government, according to James Mill, should be to secure the greatest happiness of this class.

Happiness, however, is a complex idea. What is to be the standard by which we are to measure happiness? Is the poorest class to be the judge of what will constitute their greatest happiness? Is the idea of happiness limited to earthly existence, or does it include the idea of a future life? These are questions which might perplex ordinary readers.

James Mill, however, explicity declared that the greatest happiness of the greatest number was to be attained by "insuring to every man the greatest possible quantity of the produce of his labour." The greatest number in every community must be the working class, and if every individual of that class could obtain the greatest possible quantity of the produce of his labour, the problem, in Mill's opinion, would be solved.

Having at the outset stated this as the object to be pursued, Mill founded his scheme of government upon what he believed to be the principles of human nature. Selfishness is, Mill asserted, the prevailing motive of human conduct, and the only mode of neutralizing the selfishness of a portion of the community is to allow the whole community to govern itself. This perfect form of government could, he contended, be obtained by a system of representation, the grand discovery of modern times. Universal suffrage was thus proclaimed to be the complete and final solution of the political problem.

According to this theory, all history might be discarded as useless for the purpose of political instruction. The experience derived from the study of antecedent governments was superseded by a scheme founded on the invariable principles of human nature. There could be no further question as to the distribution of political power. The mixed Constitution of this realm, and the balance of the Three Estates, were contemptuously dismissed as chimerical and absurd.

Representation, by means of universal suffrage, was propounded as the panacea for all the evils which arise from misgovernment. James Mill did not, however, pursue his theory to its logical result ; for if the evils resulting from personal selfishness can only be obviated by universal suffrage ; why were the women, that is half the community, to be excluded? Mill inconsistently excluded women from his scheme.

At the time when Mill published this treatise
there was a general desire for some expansion
and improvement of our representative system.
The large portion of active and intelligent men
of business, which in this country constitutes,
what is called, the middle class, although eager
for Parliamentary reform, were by no means
prepared for the extensive change advocated
by James Mill.   In order to conciliate this
influential class, Mill adopted the following
argument :—

" The middle class," he said, "are the most
wise and the most virtuous class in every
community, and the opinions of the people
who are below the middle rank are formed, and
their minds directed, by that intelligent and
virtuous class.   It is," he added, " altogether
futile to assert that this or any other portion
of the people may at this or at any other time
depart from the wisdom of the middle class;
it is enough that the great majority of the
people never cease to be guided by that class,

and we may with confidence challenge the adversaries of the people to produce a single instance to the contrary in the history of the world."

Fifty years in the world's history have dispelled many illusions, and if belief in the pre-eminent virtues of the middle class has been somewhat shaken, all confidence in Mill's assertion, "that the people who are below the middle rank will be invariably guided by the class above them," has been destroyed by the evidence of facts. The basis of Mill's reasoning has failed, and the theory founded upon it is worthless.

The first postulate assumed by Mill is equally untenable, namely, that "the object of all government should be to insure to every man the greatest possible quantity of the produce of his labour." The numerical majority of every community are chiefly occupied in securing daily sustenance and animal enjoyments; if the attainment of these ends constitutes the sole object of government, the result will be a degraded society, deficient in every characteristic which elevates and purifies the nature of man.

A political philosophy which assumed selfishness to be the incentive of all human actions, and adopted it as the principle on which government should be based, was the production of a cynical mind, refusing to acknowledge the intellectual and moral qualities of men, with all the various problems to which these qualities give rise.

Whatever opinion may be formed of James Mill's treatise on " Government," no intelligent person would now regard it as a satisfactory solution of the political problem.

CHAPTER V.

LORD MACAULAY'S THEORY—THE SCIENCE OF POLITICS FOUNDED ON INDUCTION.

JAMES MILL'S scheme of government was vigorously criticized by Macaulay, who argued with his usual eloquence and ability that the diversity of human nature is so great as to render all reasoning based on any one motive fallacious. Having illustrated this statement by numerous examples, Macaulay proceeded to explain the wider foundation on which, in his opinion, the science of government should be constructed. He proposed to reach it by induction—that is, " by observing the present state of the world—by assiduously studying the history of past ages—by sifting the evidence of facts—by carefully combining and contrasting those which are authentic—

by generalizing with judgment and diffidence —by perpetually bringing the theory constructed to the test of new facts—by correcting or altogether abandoning it, according as those new facts prove it to be partially or fundamentally unsound." "This," said Macaulay, "is the noble science of politics, which of all sciences is the most important to the welfare of nations, which of all sciences most tends to expand and invigorate the mind, which draws nutriment and ornament from every part of philosophy and literature, and dispenses in return nutriment and ornament to all."

Having admired this declamation, if we follow Macaulay's advice and proceed to test his theory by the evidence of facts, the system appears illusory. By induction Macaulay must be supposed to mean the process of attaining general truths by the accumulation and verification of facts.

This system, although successful in the

study of physical science, has never been
applied to politics. The British Constitution
was not the result of elaborate induction. The
Revolution of 1688 was not brought about by
generalizing with judgment and diffidence.
The conduct of King James alarmed the
country, and offended the religious feelings of
the people. The tyranny of the King led to
the treachery of his Ministers ; and a wide-
spread conspiracy was contrived by politicians,
who had no tincture of science and no scruples
of morality.

If Macaulay's theory is tested by the
measures which were contemporary with his
own public life, it will be found equally
inapplicable. The three chief measures of
that period were, the Roman Catholic Emanci-
pation, the Parliamentary Reform, and the
Repeal of the Corn Laws. Their passage
through Parliament was not the result of any
inductive reasoning, but was forced on the
Legislature by popular violence, by the

exigencies of the day, and by all the mixed motives which animate party strife.

Perhaps Macaulay did not intend to assert that political measures had been the fruit of induction, but that the science of politics should be founded on this philosophical system.

Macaulay's theory appears to be altogether erroneous when applied to the problems which living politicians desire to solve. The data on which to base inductive reasoning cannot be found.

What will constitute the best representative system ?

How can the differences between capital and labour be adjusted ?

Should the connection between the Church and State be dissolved ?

These are a few of the questions which agitate society in this country at the present time, and for their solution induction is not available.

The endeavour to found the science of politics on selfishness, which was the theory of James Mill, and the attempt by Macaulay to found this science on induction, appear to be equally inapplicable to modern communities. Buckle, in his unfinished work on the " History of Civilization," observes : " Politics, so far from being a science, is one of the most backward of all the arts, and the only safe course for the legislator is to look upon his craft as consisting in the adaptation of temporary contrivances to temporary emergencies."

Macaulay denounces the system of meeting the exigencies of the day by the expedients of the day as unworthy of statesmen ; but unfortunately the complexity of human affairs renders it impossible to employ the scientific method of reasoning which he recommends.

The strength of Radicalism was founded, not on the arguments of James Mill or of any other philosophical politician, but on the observation of the prosperity of the United States of

America. The Radicals honestly believed that the Americans owed their prosperity to their Republican form of government, This, therefore, was the model which the Radicals presented to the people of this kingdom for imitation. Every extension of the franchise would, it was hoped, tend towards this consummation.

Truth is said to be the daughter of Time; and although a century is a short period in the history of nations, yet it may assist us to form an opinion on the merits of democracy based on universal suffrage.

CHAPTER VI.

THE GREAT REPUBLIC.

THE United States of North America have now for a century presented to the world an example of a Democratic Republic on a large scale ; thus refuting the assertion of Montesquieu who said : " Il est de la nature d'une république qu'elle n'ait qu'un petit territoire, sans cella elle ne peut guère subsister."

The founders of this Constitution enjoyed every advantage which could contribute to the successful establishment of a free commonwealth. The first immigration from England may justly be ascribed to the two noblest impulses which can animate the human mind —religion and civil liberty. Genuine piety and manly independence distinguished the men who resolved to leave their native land and to encounter the perils and privations of an unknown world, in order that they might worship God according to their conscientious belief, and live or die in the wilderness as an over-ruling Providence might decree. " We came into these parts to enjoy the liberties of the gospel in purity and in peace." Such is said to have been the first declaration put forth by the ancestors of the future Republicans, and its grand simplicity of expression is certainly unsurpassed by the subsequent more pretentious Declaration of Independence. The religious enthusiasm, the austere morals, the undaunted bravery of the first settlers, qualified them to inaugurate in the New World a new era of happiness and virtue. They seemed to be guided in their exertions, and sustained in their sufferings by some holy inspiration which accompanied their voyages: " Spiritus Dei ferebatur super aquas."

When the disputes arose between the American colonies and the Mother Country—

when, as an American historian relates, "a twopenny tax on tea changed the history of the civilized world"—the independence of the states was secured by the courage, the wisdom, and the moderation of leaders, who proved themselves worthy of their noble lineage.

Victorious in their conflict, and temperate in their triumph, the colonists became at once the acknowledged masters of an unlimited territory, rich in fertility of soil and in variety of climate, abounding in mineral wealth, in navigable rivers, and in natural harbours.

Liberated from the interference of European Governments, and released from the prejudices of the Old World, the Americans could now establish for themselves a political society, which might develop the highest faculties of man, and exhibit to astonished nations the most perfect scheme of civilized life. In the process of constructing their Government the American statesmen do not appear to have been hampered by their celebrated Declaration

of Independence, in which " all men were pronounced to be equal, and endowed by their
Maker with inalienable rights." No concession
of rights to the negro or to the Indian—to the
black man or to the red man, was mentioned.
The statesmen wisely discarded the Declaration
of Independence as a mere political manifesto
which had served its purpose; and they proceeded to establish safeguards against the
ambition of public functionaries and against the
capricious decisions of the sovereign people.

In the construction of the Constitution
differences of opinion arose as to the proper
distribution of political power. Alexander
Hamilton contended for safeguards against the
aggressive encroachments of the poorest class,
while Jefferson supported the claims of the
popular party. In this contest the opinions of
Jefferson prevailed, and subsequently, when he
became President of the United States, he
contributed still further to develop the principles of the democratic government.

It was the fortune of Jefferson to be present at the birth of two republics : in America and in France. The statesmen of America, while they retained the local administration of the provincial legislatures, united the several states in a Federal Government, which they framed upon a pattern in some respects analogous to the Constitution of the Mother Country. Their political arrangements displayed much practical wisdom ; and although further experience has brought to light many defects, yet the result was successful in the establishment of communities destined eventually to become a free and powerful commonwealth.

The politicians of France rejecting all past experience boasted that they would regenerate the civilized world on the principles of the rights of man, of fraternity, and equality. The result ended in military despotism and in the failure of their lofty aspirations. Jefferson, writing on the condition of France, towards the close of his own life, expressed his sorrow that the Republic had ended in despotism, and that, after millions of lives had been sacrificed in war, with all its attendant miseries, the fabric of Liberty was in ruins, and the odious monarchs remained sitting in triumph on their re-established thrones.

The correspondence of Jefferson has fortunately been preserved, and we can now compare the condition of a democratic community, which has endured for a hundred years, with the confident predictions of a man who was the chief author of the existing Constitution.

Jefferson had an unhesitating faith in the perfectibility of mankind through the operation of democratic institutions. He believed that kings and aristocracies were the only obstacles to the development of human virtue, and that the moral nature of man, when emancipated from these vicious tyrants, would be at once renovated and purified in the atmosphere of freedom. He could only speak of kings as pestilent monsters, and the words of Voltaire's tragedy would exactly represent his sentiments,

" Je suis fils de Brutus, et je porte en mon cœur
La liberté gravée, et les rois en horreur."

So deeply impressed was he with the dangerous and immoral influence of kingly governments and of aristocratic society, that he objected to young Americans visiting Europe, " lest," as he says, " they should acquire the taste for luxury and dissipation prevalent in the capitals of the Old World."

In another letter, he contrasts "the voluptuous dress and arts of European women with the chaste affections and inartificial manners which would be found in the United States."

Contemplating in his imagination American society in future years as a perpetual feast of intellectual pleasure and of unalloyed virtue, Jefferson ventured to predict : "No man living will ever see an instance of an American removing to settle in Europe, while we shall see multiplied instances of Europeans going to live in America."

It is amusing to read this prediction by the light of recent days. Whilst few Europeans settle in America, unless driven there by lack of money or of character, many Americans flocked to the cities of Europe, and specially selected Paris as their home, not during its Republican rule, but while it was the seat of Imperial power. Educated Americans gladly escaped from the vulgar monotony of a community absorbed in money-making, to a capital which, after many convulsions, still retained traces of its traditional culture and refinement.

Jefferson seems to have believed that the establishment of a republic would at once resuscitate the primitive society which he had studied in the school-room; and that the new world would again behold the matronly pride of a Cornelia, the rustic frugality of a Cincinnatus, and the unimpeachable integrity of a Fabricius.

Reasoning from what he knew of ancient Athens, he imagined that a finished and chastened purity of taste, refining literature and art, would soften the manners of his countrymen, and render society in America irresistibly attractive.

A democratic government has, it may be said, higher purposes in view than to cultivate the amenities and polished manners of social life. Republican institutions, Jefferson argued, would assuredly generate the sterner virtues of integrity and justice.

There is abundant evidence that here also Jefferson was in error. The American Constitution has not produced superior honesty in the conduct of commercial business, or in the administration of public affairs. The vices of the Old World seem to sprout up with increased luxuriance in the new soil. The extent and variety of commercial frauds disclose a very lax morality in the trading communities of the United States. Whether this is the result of

democratic institutions, or of the many inducements to financial speculation in a country where
mercantile enterprise reaps the richest harvest,
cannot be affirmed without further experience
and observation.

Lord Brougham, writing in the year 1843,
upon American Democracy, asserted that the
vigilance of parties and "the publicity with
which every department of government is
administered, make peculation impossible. It
is an offence" he said "which in such a country
can have no existence."

Further experience and public trials have
proved that a democratic government affords
in itself no sufficient security against peculation, embezzlement, and official malver-
sation.

Maladministration of the law through the
dishonesty of the judges was one of the worst
vices of arbitrary government, but this vice has
not been eradicated by democracy. The courts
of justice, even the legislatures, are tainted

with venality, and the public service is mono-
polized by an oligarchy of place-holders and
place-seekers, who manage and manipulate
elections and appointments for their own
selfish advantage.

These lamentable results of unrestricted
democracy do not prevent the rapid increase
of material prosperity. An honest administration of the law is preferable, but it is not
indispensable to the acquisition of wealth.
The incorruptibility of public functionaries
dignifies the character of a nation, but communities have often attained great power and
opulence amidst much social and political
corruption.

The whole construction of the American
Constitution seems calculated to maintain a
low standard of moral integrity. From the
highest position in the state to the lowest
appointment, the inducements to practise or
to profit by corruption are innumerable.
Instances of commercial dishonesty may be

found in every country, but in the United
States, flagrant cases of fraud are hardly
viewed with disapprobation.

Every thing in the United States is com-
mensurate with the magnitude of its territory,
and pecuniary corruption has assumed gigantic
dimensions.

The two great parties which have alternately
ruled the country agree in maintaining that
all the public offices, from the presidency
downwards, are the prizes of political victory.
The result has been, as was foretold by
Alexander Hamilton, that the political energies
of the whole people are absorbed in the contest
for the next presidency. The president, moreover, can be re-elected. He therefore employs
the immense patronage at his disposal, and
all the machinery of administration, to secure
a new lease of office. The practical result
is, that the Americans, in their determination
to discard monarchy, have set up a ruler
with some of the worst attributes of personal

government. Instead of being above party, and the moderator of conflicting factions, the president is the keenest of partisans. He must reward his political adherents for their past allegiance, and bribe them for the next election. Unless he misuses his power he dissatisfies his party, and the interests of the country are subordinate to the gratification of his supporters.

Three years of perpetual canvass, with an army of a hundred thousand eager office-holders and office-seekers, whose appointments depend on the single will of the president, are sufficient to corrupt a nation. And the nation is corrupted. Thus the politics of the great Republic end in a subjection of four years' duration to a ruler who must distribute the emoluments of office amongst his greedy followers; and with every new president a new scramble commences.

It must be observed, in justice to the memory of Jefferson, that he disapproved the constitutional law which made a president re-eligible.

The alteration of this law would perhaps be attended with some benefit, but such a change would not of itself suffice to purify the public service.

John Stuart Mill, in his review of Bentham's Political Writings, observed, " The numerical majority of any community must consist of persons in the same social position, namely, manual labourers. These persons will be influenced by the same desires, passions, and prejudices. If supreme power is lodged in this class, with no corrective force to counteract its exercise, the whole fabric of society will be impressed and moulded in this one mean type of human nature."

This is unfortunately the position of the United States. The educated class of Americans, who in culture and refinement are on a level with the best society of Europe, stand aloof from the political contests of the states, and look down with contempt on the audacious managers of an electoral machinery which is worked by fraud and falsehood.

Under such a system it is not surprising that political life has deteriorated. The statesmen and orators of the last century have been succeeded by men, whose insignificance excites no democratic jealousy at home, and who are unknown abroad, except when some outrageous scandal attracts the notice of the European press. It has been truly said, "When the United States contained only three million inhabitants, they produced men whose fame will live as long as the English language. Now there is not a single man of distinction in thirty millions. Every president is inferior to his predecessor."

It is now a period of forty years since Tocqueville published his observations on democracy in America.

"Voulez vous donner à l'esprit humain une certaine hauteur, une façon généreuse d'envisager les choses de ce monde ? Voulez vous inspirer aux hommes une sorte de mépris des biens matériels ? Désirez vous faire naître ou entretenir des convictions profondes et préparer de grands devouemens ? S'agit il de polir les mœurs, d'élever les manières, de faire briller les arts ? Si tel est, suivant vous, l'objet principal que doivent se proposer les hommes en société, ne prenez pas le gouvernement de la démocratie, il ne conduirait pas sûrement au but.

" Mais s'il vous semble utile de détourner l'activité intellectuelle et morale de l'homme sur les nécessités de la vie matérielle et dé l'employer a produire le bien-être, alors constituez le gouvernement de la démocratie."

It would seem that all the noblest results of civilization, the amenities of social life, the refinement of taste, the cultivation of the arts which elevate and dignify mankind, are to be relinquished for the sake of promoting the well-being of the working man, the animal existence of the manual labourer. Has this object been attained ? Is the working man in the United States satisfied and contented ? Is there no jealousy of the capitalist ? Are there not trades - unions and associations, whose object it is to regulate wages without reference to supply and demand ?

Tocqueville believed that democratic insti-tutions would promote the material well-being and the animal enjoyments of the community. He saw around him an intelligent and energetic people in a new country of unlimited extent, where surrounding circumstances, not only stimulated, but compelled them to exertion; and he argued : "this energetic industry and con-sequent prosperity are the fruits of democracy ; the United States are the paradise of working men." Subsequent experience has proved that even in a republic with universal suffrage there is no permanent security for that comfortable existence which was the promised consum-mation of democratic institutions. The working man has found depression of trade and scarcity of employment restricting his wages. He sees, moreover, profuse wealth and vulgar plutocracy towering over him, and flaunting their dishonest gains in the face of his discontented penury. Tocqueville predicted that in the United States there would be a tendency to the equalization of wealth ; the rich would gradually become poorer, and the poor become richer. This prediction has been refuted by the course of events. There is no country where private fortunes are larger, or where the power of capital has been more invidiously exerted.

The conflict between labour and capital has burst forth in destructive riots, has engaged the sympathies of the poorer classes in several states, and there is as yet no sign of a reconciliation or peaceable adjustment of these unseemly disputes.

Has the great Republic opened a new era of virtue and happiness to mankind? Has it ennobled the national character and raised the moral tone of society? Does it afford an example of magnanimity and of a delicate sense of honour in transactions with other states?

Those persons who hoped for such results will turn away from the United States with feelings of disappointment and humiliation. It would lead us to despair of human nature, if we believed that this form of government would be the last and highest effort of civilization.

There is, however, a serious difficulty in the amendment of a Constitution based on universal suffrage. Such a democracy is in one sense eminently conservative; it would assuredly offer vigorous resistance to any change. A monarchy may be limited by law or by prescription; an aristocracy may be deprived of its powers and privileges; but a democracy, when once it is supreme, howsoever degraded its character, or arbitrary its conduct, can only be dethroned by a military

6 *

revolution. In this case the remedy would be worse than the disease.

It is, however, idle to speculate on the future.

" Futuri temporis exitum
Caliginosâ nocte premit Deus."

CHAPTER VII.

THE WORKING OF REPRESENTATIVE INSTITUTIONS.

A FEELING is manifesting itself among thoughtful politicians, both in Europe and America, that the practical working of representative institutions is not altogether satisfactory. In the present condition of the most civilized states, constitutional government affords the best security for the orderly conduct of the community and for the prudent administration of public affairs. Representation is an essential element of constitutional government. The object of an electoral system should be to bring together a body of men who would represent the deliberate sense and conscience of the nation.

For this purpose it is neither necessary nor

desirable that the representatives should reflect every transient shadow or momentary wave of opinion which may pass over the surface of society. Such a system of representation would weaken the executive government by producing instability in the policy of the state, and a general feeling of uncertainty and distrust.

On the other hand, if the representative body is widely separated from the mass of the people, it ceases to be a faithful interpreter of the national mind. Public confidence is then withdrawn, and the whole system of the Constitution is impaired.

Some intermediate position between these two extremes should be the object of a sound representative system.

By whatever mode of election a body of educated persons are chosen as members of a representative assembly, an echo of public opinion will be heard amongst them. In this country a system of representation proportioned to population, to property, to taxation, or to any other intelligible basis, never existed. The whole electoral machinery was composed of anomalies and incongruities.

Before the Reform Act of 1832, many large towns throughout the country, the centres of industry and wealth, were excluded from representation; whilst the aristocratic patron, the jobbing borough-monger, the self-elected corporation, the venal freeman, and the drunken pot-walloper, nominated a considerable proportion of the House of Commons.

Nevertheless, this constituent body, in spite of the intrigues of courtiers and place-men, raised the first Pitt to power, and sustained him in his vigorous and victorious administration. It enabled the second Pitt to defeat a clever but dishonest coalition, and to appeal, with triumphant success, from Parliament to the nation. In subsequent years this imperfect constituent body proved itself a faithful interpreter of public opinion by giving a persistent

and patriotic support to a Government engaged
in a tremendous conflict for European freedom,
and eventually raised this kingdom to a predominance which reformed constituencies have
never equalled.

Until a late period in the history of this
country, a real representation of the majority
of the people would have been a national
calamity. Even in the early part of the
eighteenth century—when science and literature
were cultivated with success by distinguished
authors—the great mass of the people were still
in such a condition of fanatical ignorance, that
they would gladly have persecuted the Dissenters and restored the Stuarts. It would,
indeed, be easy to show that during the greater
part of the last century the sense of the whole
nation, if it had been duly represented, would
have been an untrustworthy director of the
national policy.

Are we, then, quite certain that a future

generation will not reject with contempt the political sentiments which are now shouted in market-places or applauded in town-halls ?

The system of representative institutions is based upon the principle that the constituent body reflects the collective wisdom of the nation.   Radicals maintain that all persons, both men and women (excluding minors, criminals, and lunatics), should form the constituent body.   It is even affirmed, by straining the usual meaning of language, that persons debarred from the exercise of the franchise are virtually slaves.

According to this political theory, the majority of the whole people, without reference to property, to taxation, to education, or to sex, should elect the representatives.

Government by party is the inseparable accompaniment of representative institutions. The rivalry of competing parties seeking popular support will continually tend to enlarge the constituent body.   Thus it appears that uni-

versal suffrage (or a suffrage nearly universal)
is the ultimate and unavoidable result of
representative reforms.

When representation has descended to the
lowest stratum of society, it can fall no further.

" Qui jacet in terrâ non habet unde cadat."

What will be the possible consequences to
the British Empire of such an extension of the
franchise ?

The political affairs of the Empire in this
nineteenth century are more complex than
those of any other state in ancient or modern
times. The geographical position of this island,
which, according to the Roman poet, detached
it from the rest of the world, now, on the
contrary, connects it with every region of the
habitable globe. No other state was ever
governed under such an anomalous mixture of
monarchical and democratic institutions. No
other state ever possessed so many distant
dependencies ruled under such various systems

of administration. The interests of this
country are so diversified, intricate, and entangled by commercial and financial ties, so
interwoven with the credit of foreign states,
that the least disturbance in any part of the
world immediately vibrates here, producing
embarrassment and alarm.

This artificial condition of society is to be
subjected to the capricious decisions of ignorant
and needy electors enfranchised by universal
suffrage.

CHAPTER VIII.

THE POLITICS OF THE PROLETARIAT.

CICERO, in his treatise, "De Re Publica," says, in describing the divisions of the Roman tribes by Servius Sulpicius: "Eos, qui nihil in suum censum præter caput attulissent proletarios nominavit, ut ex iis proles, id est quasi progenies civitatis expectari videretur."

The word "proletariat" has been accordingly used to signify the poorest class of labourers or artisans. These men, passing their lives in monotonous occupation, seldom exercise their mental faculties. They possess little individuality of character, and feeble powers of discrimination. As a class, they are generous one to another, and readily sympathize with their fellow-workmen, whenever trades-unionism does

not debase and poison their moral temperament.

They are deficient in self-control, and are
easily excited by preachers or speakers, who
have the skill to touch their feelings, or to
inflame their passions. They naturally desire
to increase their wages and to lessen their
labour. Their daily necessities pre-occupy
their thoughts, and they are ill-qualified
to take an enlarged view even of their
own interests, still less of the affairs of the
nation.

Crowded meetings of workmen are more fit
for the rough labour of demolition than for the
elaborate task of construction. To this end,
therefore, their energies have usually been
directed by demagogues in ancient as well as
in modern times.

It is not without some feelings of solicitude
that we shall see this numerous class legally
established as the guardians of the British
Empire, and the custodians of that constitu-

tional edifice which it has taken ages to build up.

These men, although incompetent to decide upon many complex questions of politics, might pronounce a just opinion on a matter fairly submitted to their judgment, but political meetings are not favourable to the calm consideration of men or of measures.

CHAPTER IX.

" Ce sont deux animaux bien bêtes que l'homme et le lapin
une fois qu'ils sont pris par les oreilles."

LE MARQUIS DE MIRABEAU.

THE art of leading men by their ears, which
the elder Mirabeau professed to despise, the
younger Mirabeau practised with signal success.

In this country at party gatherings the art is
simplified, inasmuch as the speeches are only
addressed to partisans. Argument is superfluous
when the hearers are already convinced—when
they only meet to be flattered for their wisdom,
and to applaud the condemnation of their
opponents.

Exaggerated language, reckless statements,
scornful denunciations, imputations of dishonesty and stupidity, are the chief ingredients
of these speeches. It would not be difficult to

cull an anthology of vituperative phrases from the flowery eloquence with which at these meetings even statesmen gratify their adherents.

These assemblies tend to corrupt both orator and auditory. The orator mistakes the cheers of heated partisans for the expression of public opinion; the auditory are inflamed with animosities, and rendered incapable of exercising such reasoning faculties as they may possess.

For the purpose of diffusing political knowledge, and preparing the class of working-men for a more direct participation in the government of the state, these gatherings are worse than useless.

Lamartine (who was himself a proficient in this style of oratory) wrote in his " Histoire des Girondins" :—" Pour passioner les peuples il faut qu'un peu d'illusion se mêle à la verité; la realité seule est trop froide pour fanatiser l'esprit humain."

In all accumulations of animal matter there is an immediate tendency to ferment, and a crowd of human beings is especially liable to this effervescence. History records the fanatical and tumultuous riots of populous cities, and it is often noticed that the most numerous urban constituencies are the most unreasonable.

When men of business are engaged in conducting commercial affairs, and in managing large trading establishments, they endeavour to reason calmly, and to resist the impulses of passion and of rivalry. But when they address themselves to the consideration of public affairs, which are more complex and difficult of solution, they endeavour to stir every passion which lurks in the human breast.

" Il faut hurler avec les loups," is a proverb which is adopted as the device of the spouters who pour out these frothy declamations to win the applause of the working men. While acknowledging the success of these harangues, the impartial bystander will be inclined to say, with a late Prime Minister, " I stand in awe of the power of falsehood."

It seems probable that this country will be kept in a condition of political agitation and unrest until a franchise so widely extended as to be nearly universal has been established. The experience of universal suffrage in other countries is not encouraging, and able writers have suggested measures to neutralize, or at least to mitigate, the ill-effects of transferring political power from the educated to the ignorant and indigent classes of the community.

One remedy is the education of the people. On this subject a few words will be said hereafter.

.The other remedy consists in some rearrangement of the electoral machinery, or even a reconstruction of the whole representative system. Assuming mere numbers to be

the basis of representation, various schemes
have been proposed, which may be enumerated
under the following queries :

Should the whole electoral body be allowed
to divide itself arbitrarily, and elect ?

Should there be electoral districts ?

If so ; what should constitute an electoral
district ?

Should each district elect one member or
more ?

If more than one member, how many ?

Here questions arise as to the limited vote,
the plurality vote, the cumulative vote, and
other intricate contrivances, which are called
scientific by their ingenious inventors, and
denounced as fanciful theories by impatient
politicians.

Whether the present haphazard system of
representation be retained, or another system
substituted, the machinery of elections will
always be so cumbrous and complicated that
it will require to be regulated or guided by

7 *

skilled managers. These managers will be party tools, selected, after much intrigue and local jealousy, to do the dirty work of politics. They will manipulate the electors, and, in communication with some central committee, consider how to win the seat in the House of Commons. The fitness of the candidate to be a member of Parliament is of course an entirely subordinate question.

The result will be that, in most cases, after all the trouble and expense of this electoral apparatus, from the registration to the final ballot, the system resolves itself into a circuitous mode of nominating members of Parliament by a small body of managers.

One effect of this system will be that a large proportion of sensible and moderate men will abstain from voting. They will be aware that, unless they vote according to the dictate of a managing committee, their votes will be thrown away.

That portion of the electors, whose calm

judgment and temperate disposition would supply a counterpoise to the violence of party warfare, will stand aloof; and the country will lose the beneficial influence of that body of men who are best qualified to weigh the value of antagonistic opinions, and to take a correct survey of the political horizon.

This is an evil which appears to be insepara-ble from a widely extended franchise.

CHAPTER X.

EDUCATION THE SAFEGUARD OF SOCIETY.

THE education of the people is now a national charge, and a recognized duty of the state. Various motives, religious, charitable and political, have contributed to this result. There is, however, some delusion as to the political effects of popular education.

Tocqueville, in his book on " Democracy in America," pointed out the dangers which threaten European civilization from the multitudes of needy and ignorant men who regard the institutions of civilized society as unjustifiable usurpations. He expressed a hope, although with some diffidence, that a system of education (in which he included a course of religious instruction) might afford a safeguard against an irruption of savage passions and brutal violence such as France had witnessed after the Revolution of 1789.

The language of Tocqueville on this im-portant matter is not reassuring. He knew that the questions which agitate the poorest class involve some of the most difficult problems of social life. A lecture on political economy will not appease an empty stomach; and elementary education, while it may open to a few vigorous intellects the vestibule of literature and science, appears to produce in the children of the poor very inadequate results, as com-pared with the expectations of some amiable philanthropists. Forty years have elapsed since Tocqueville stated his views on the education which he desired to see as an established system in European countries.

" Instruire la démocratie, r'animer, s'il se peut, ses croyances, purifier ses mœurs, régler ses mouvemens, substituer peu à peu la science des affaires à son inexpérience, la connaissance

de ses vrais interêts à ses aveugles instincts,"
&c. &c.

At the very time when this book was published the French Government were occupied
in providing a system of national education.
They commenced by instituting preliminary
inquiries as to the systems of popular education
adopted in other countries. M. Cousin was
sent to investigate the schools of Germany and
Switzerland, and on his report a grand scheme
of national education was submitted to the
French Chamber. In introducing this measure
the Minister ventured to predict from the
adoption of the plan a new era of glory for the
French nation. "Increased knowledge would,"
he said, " dispel the illusions which credulity
had fostered, disorder would be repressed by an
enlightened public opinion, the populace would
disappear, and be replaced by an intelligent and
moral people; society would then be founded
on a secure basis, and the future condition of
France would realise the promises which the
Revolution of 1789 had failed to fulfil."

The French Chamber accepted the measure ;
a liberal allowance was granted for its establishment, and M. Cousin was appointed Minister
of Public Instruction. In this system of education religious teaching occupied a prominent
place. M. Cousin was even bitterly reproached
by his former admirers for having conceded so
much to the clergy.

The Government of France under Louis
Philippe was specially qualified to establish an
enlightened system of education. Not only
had the King himself acquired some experience
in the teaching of youth, but his Ministry contained several distinguished authors and professors; Guizot, Villemain, Thiers, Cousin, Barante,
constituted a dazzling galaxy of writers such
as no other Government could exhibit.

The observation of Pliny might at that
period have been applied to the French
ministers :—" Quos tibi, fortuna, ludos facis,
facis enim ex professoribus senatores, ex
senatoribus professores."

The educational movement in France attracted immediate notice in England, and motions for the appointment of a Minister of Education were made in Parliament. In this country legislative movements are usually slow; and although money was voted for the encouragement of schools, and annually increasing grants were made for educational purposes, yet forty years elapsed before the British Government undertook a general ·scheme of national education.

In considering the probable effects of education as a political safeguard, it is not unreasonable to examine into the results of education in France and in other countries.

The condition of France during the last forty years has not fulfilled the promises predicted by the Ministers of Louis Philippe. Education has not dissipated social delusions or repressed disorder. So far from having produced these benefits, education seems to have stimulated the discontent which it was intended to counteract. The intelligent artisans, the skilled workmen, are found to be the most turbulent members of the community. The more ignorant peasantry are peaceful and orderly, while the chief manufacturing towns are the centres of political disquietude.

Is the system of education defective? Or are there in France other impulses which neutralize the beneficial results which were so confidently anticipated?

Guizot, in his lectures on " Civilization," asserted that common sense is the distinctive characteristic of the French people. " Le bon sens est le trait distinctif du génie Français."

Without implicitly accepting this statement, it will be readily admitted that the French people are singularly quick of apprehension, and capable of the highest intellectual culture.

Before the Revolution of 1789 they occupied a foremost place among the nations of Europe in literature, in science, and in all the arts and amenities of civilized life.

In more recent years, although the material

prosperity of France has increased, her political condition has not advanced with equal rapidity.

The French nation accepted constitutional monarchy, reduced the nobility to mere names, abolished primogeniture, restricted the freedom of bequest, deprived the Church of her ancient possessions, and established a system of popular education; nevertheless, after all these radical measures, the people were discontented, despised their Citizen King, sighed for " la Gloire," and wished to be again the predominant power in Europe.

If the French people have learnt moderation, the lesson has been impressed on their minds, not by school-instruction, but by the disasters of war and the severe penalties of defeat.

Even now, however, they welcome with applause the returned Communists, the men who destroyed their public edifices, who wished to obliterate the monuments of their historical fame, and to subject French society to another revolution.

Has education produced tranquillity and social contentment in Germany? Are not the wildest theories rife among the workmen, perplexing the Government, and even disturbing the legislature. America, however, is often cited as a proof of the peaceable influence of popular education.

Education in the United States of America has not proved to be the panacea for the evils which there also disturb the happiness of social life. In the Report on the Industrial Conflicts which occurred in the year 1877, the opinion of an American writer is recorded, and deserves the attention of educationists in this country.

"What a terrible satire upon our boasted free-school system is conveyed in the word 'educated.' Nine-tenths of the young criminals sent to the Penitentiary have enjoyed school advantages, but three-fourths have never learnt to do an honest stroke of work. Our children have their poor little brains crammed full of all kinds of knowledge, of names, and dates, and numbers, until there is absolutely no room left to hold any of the simple truths of honour, duty, and morality, which former generations deemed more important than all the learning of the books. The result is, that they leave school utterly ignorant of all that is most essential for them to know; and outside of the schools there is no provision for learning anything."

The Americans have, however, incitements to education which the poor in this country do not possess. The immense territory and variety of climate afford opportunities for diversified experience, which quickens the mental faculties to a degree unattainable under the monotony of old-established communities.

Lord Bacon (in his great work, " De Augmentis") pointed out the deficiencies of education, and suggested that philosophers should endeavour to ascertain the effects produced by different modes of education, by continuous

training of the mental faculties, and by generating a healthy habit of disposition.

In considering the education of the poorest
class it must always be remembered that every
child is subject to two different systems of
mental training; the system in school, and the
system out of school. The children of the
poor attend the school for a few hours, and
then return to their homes. If these homes
contaminate the youthful mind with the coarse
and debasing associations too common amongst
the lowest class of working-men, the school
teaching may sharpen the intellect, but it will be
powerless to counteract the habitual influence
of domestic life.

The children of the poor are not subjected
to the continuous discipline which is an important part of the education of other classes.
They may be taught to answer questions learned
by rote, and even to perform some feats in
arithmetic; but for the acquisition of political
knowledge, and as a security for the peace and

good order of society, it would be a delusion to rely upon the education which can be imparted during a few years of childhood.

So far as an opinion can be formed from the results of education in Europe and in America, no reliance can be placed on school instruction as a safeguard of society.

This statement is not a reason for depriving the poor of elementary education, which is indispensable under the conditions of modern life.

The probable effects, however, will not be to promote contentment, or to facilitate the orderly government of the community.

The poor, when they have acquired some superficial instruction, which is all that the great majority of the working class can hope to attain, usually become violent partisans, and adopt very positive opinions on the most doubtful questions of politics.

While thoughtful politicians hesitate as to what are the proper functions of government, the poor clamour for legislative interference, looking only to the immediate result.

Human society is as yet in an early stage of its political growth; and the most complex problems of life are still unsolved.

It is worth a few minutes' attention to examine how far opinions have fluctuated in regard to some of the most interesting questions which have been the special study of political writers. Where philosophers and statesmen have erred, is it to be expected that the village schoolmaster will set the world to rights?

CHAPTER XI.

THE FUNCTIONS OF THE GOVERNMENT.

WHAT are the proper functions of the governing power? Where the authority of the state should interfere, and where it should abstain from interference? These are questions intimately connected with political economy, with civil liberty, and with the whole framework of society.

The legislation of recent years seems to indicate that politicians have no settled opinion upon these questions, and are guided by no principle. The system of administration which was in former centuries regarded as profound statesmanship, was, at a later period, rejected and denounced as an unwise and mischievous policy; while the practice of modern ministers is to revert to a system of interference tending to control and regulate the whole life and freedom of the subject.

Which system is best calculated to promote the welfare of the nation is a problem, which the science of politics, if such a science exists, should enable us to solve.

In former centuries the English Government, like other European states, assumed itself to be pre-eminent in wisdom as in power, and undertook to direct the whole course of the national life. The first and most important function was to prescribe the religious belief and devotional ceremonies of the people. This function was approved by the wisest statesmen, and was in harmony with the public opinion of that age. The Government, moreover, attempted to regulate the occupations of the people, and even the details of domestic management. Sumptuary laws were passed to repress the luxury of the rich, and even to fix their dress and diet. Other enactments appointed the rate of wages, the price of food, and the labour to be performed.   The industry of every artisan was subject to the control of a guild and a magistrate.   Commerce was restricted; and with the view of increasing the national wealth, the export of the precious metals was prohibited.   The irrepressible growth of London, instead of being regarded as a proof of national prosperity, was deemed an excrescence which the law might usefully check.

This system of public policy was sanctioned by the great name of Bacon, who was not only himself instrumental in furthering such legislation, but who also, as an historian of the reign of Henry VII, lauded the statesmanship of that king for enforcing measures of a similar character.

A later generation of statesmen introduced an entirely opposite policy.   They contended that the interference of the state in the details of private life and of industrial occupations was both unjust and mischievous.   All government was a restriction of human liberty, and should only be enforced where it was indispensable. Over-governing, it was now said, had been the bane of trade and the ruin of manufactures. The proper course was to repeal these vexatious enactments, and to give the freest scope to human energy. In short, all people should be allowed to manage their affairs in their own way, so long as they did not interfere with the equal liberty of their neighbours.

Freedom of conscience, freedom of the press, freedom of contract, freedom of trade, were now declared to be the true principles of an enlightened government, which should never interfere further than the exigencies of the state might require.

The celebrated book of Adam Smith confirmed a change of opinion which was already making its way among the educated classes. He limited the duties of government to those functions which can only be adequately discharged by the state itself. To these alone, he declared, should the public revenue be applied. These functions are :

1. The defence of the country against foreign enemies.

2. The security of property and tranquillity within the realm.

3. The support of the chief magistrate and of the administrative and judicial departments.

4. The collection of revenue for these purposes.

5. The expense of contributing towards the maintenance of institutions for education and religious instruction.

6. The expense of contributing to such public works as are directly beneficial to the whole community.

These two last heads of expenditure might, Adam Smith suggested, with equal propriety and with some advantage, be defrayed by those persons who derive the chief benefit from such expenditure.

Here was a definite policy, which simplified the functions of government and the labours of the legislature. For many years this policy was regarded as the true principle of administration, and the criterion of sound statesmanship.

The spirit of modern legislation has departed from the general principles propounded by Adam Smith; and after much discussion, an opposite practice has gradually prevailed.

The government is now required to interfere in almost every industrial occupation. The state is appointed to act as the guardian of the feeble, the protector of the poor, the instructor of the ignorant. Freedom of contract is no longer the ruling principle between the employer and the employed. Men are not allowed to manage their own business in their own way. Parents are not entrusted to bring up their own children. The hours of instruction and the hours of labour are regulated by law, and made matter of report to Parliament

The working man, whether he is up in the factory, down in the mine, or out on the sea, is still under the superintending eye of the government.

To secure the health of the people is now the duty of the state. The food which they eat, the water they drink (if they do drink water), and the air they breathe, must be freed from contamination. Their dwellings must be inspected, cleansed, and over-crowding prevented. The recreation of the people also occupies the attention of a benevolent legislature; but even in their holidays they must be treated as if they were children, and guarded against temptations which they are powerless to resist.

New departments are created, or old departments re-organized, with scientific inspectors, for the due performance of these multifarious functions.

The admonitions of a former generation of statesmen against what was called over-governing, are now no longer uttered, and the people are taught to believe that it is the duty of the government to secure them a comfortable existence.

When once the principles laid down by Adam Smith are rejected, it becomes difficult to define the proper limits to the interference of the state. The feelings of humanity, of charity, and of religion prompt politicians to enact new laws for the restriction of excessive toil, and for the relief of that portion of the people who are least able to protect themselves.

It is now manifest that Adam Smith based his propositions on insufficient data. A rigid adherence to his principles of government would have occasioned intolerable suffering to a large class of the population.

The authority of illustrious names has too frequently retarded the progress of science, and misguided the policy of statesmen. When experience has refuted their dogmatic decisions, the mass of mankind are apt to run into the opposite extreme, until another evil is the result.

Thus continued interference by the state undermines and destroys the habit of self-reliance, which is essential to the independence and mental energy of man. There is a striking inconsistency in assuming that the working man is incapable to take care of himself, while at the same time he is qualified to direct the policy of the state, and to control the destinies of the Empire !

It must, moreover, be remembered that laws restricting labour, however favourable they may at first seem to the health and happiness of the workmen, tend inevitably to increase the cost of production, and to diminish the profits of business. These laws may be innocuous so long as local advantages or scientific superiority enable the workmen to defy competition, but they will become injurious when the rivalry of foreign countries transfers the trade to a community content with harder work and lower wages.

Then the enactments intended to benefit the working-class have the effect of closing the workshop and depriving the workman of employment.

While statesmen are perplexed and politicians are debating these intricate problems of human life, it is not surprising that workmen should have recourse to a solution which may seem to offer a temporary benefit to themselves.

If Bacon was in error, and Adam Smith misled his followers, a working man cannot justly be blamed for misunderstanding the extent to which the principles of political economy should be applied or modified, amid the complex arrangements of modern society.

Even the question of civil liberty is as yet clouded in a haze of words, and has seldom been carefully considered by political writers.

CHAPTER XII.

OF LIBERTY.

ACCORDING to Locke, "Natural liberty consists in freedom from any superior power on earth;" or in other words, "Not to be under the will or legislative authority of man, but to be under the law of nature."

What Locke meant by the law of nature is not clear. Perhaps he was thinking of Dryden's noble savage running wild in woods. Whatever opinion Locke may have formed of what he called "natural liberty," it had no connection with politics.

Locke's explanation of civil liberty is not much more satisfactory.

"Civil liberty," he says, "is a condition wherein man is under no other legislative power but that established, by consent, in the commonwealth."

This definition confuses the reader with notions of some imaginary commonwealth, where men and women met together and consented to a code of laws. Locke was apparently dreaming of some original contract such as the English Parliament solemnly affirmed James II to have violated.

When political philosophers sanction such fictions, it is not surprising that the science of government makes little progress. It would be a waste of time to refer to many other writers whose ideas of liberty are equally indefinite and confused.

We have, however, the advantage of possessing a treatise on civil liberty written by a Radical politician, the late John Stuart Mill. It is not unreasonable to expect from a distinguished author, who expounded both politics and logic, an accurate explanation of civil liberty.

Mill commences by declaring civil liberty to consist in the personal freedom of every individual, so far as it is compatible with the freedom of other members of society. He then proceeds to explain the extent of this qualification. Mill would allow the greatest latitude to every man for the promulgation of any opinions on religion or on government. "All men," he says, "should be free to discuss the principles upon which human society is based, and to question the propriety of any institutions, although sanctified by religion and accepted by general concurrence." Mill, being himself an author, would grant entire freedom to authors. The general proposition that in every community a man should be allowed to promulgate any opinions, whatever may be their effect upon the peace and good order of society, is a statement which practical politicians will hardly admit as indispensable to civil liberty. Personal liberty must be so far restricted as not to endanger the fabric of society, or to offend the public opinion of a nation. In proposing to abolish this restriction without regard to the religious or political condition of the community, Mill surely violates the " greatest happiness principle" by permitting the annoyance of one's neighbour and provoking an outbreak of resentment.

But to proceed with the examination of this remarkable treatise.

Mill further explains personal freedom, " so far as it is consistent with the freedom of other members of society," and his explanation of liberty is so remarkable, that it must be stated in his own words :—

" In a country," Mill said, " which is over-peopled, or threatened with being so, to produce children beyond a very small number with the effect of reducing the reward of labour by their competition, is a serious offence against all who live by the remuneration of their labour. The laws which in many countries on the Continent forbid marriage, unless the

parties can show that they have means of
supporting a family, do not exceed the legitimate powers of the state ; and whether such
laws be expedient or not—a question mainly
dependent on local circumstances—they are not
objectionable as violations of liberty."

This is a startling qualification of civil
liberty propounded by a Radical philosopher.
It is also a strange misuse of words by a
logician who insists on precision of language
as essential to correct reasoning.

A law which would forbid marriage in a
country where the chief authority of the state
pronounces the territory to be overpeopled,
or threatened with being so, is asserted by
Mill to be no violation of civil liberty.

A law which would favour the rich and
punish the poor, regulating society by the
invidious test of wealth, and establishing a
property qualification for marriage is declared
to be perfectly consistent with liberty. Mill's
announcement to the assembled nations who

are eagerly asking for political liberty is to this effect, " You may produce books, as many as you please, but you must not produce children."

After reading this theory of civil liberty, it will be felt as a merciful dispensation that the world is not governed by political philosophers.

Mill would have restricted the numbers in order to increase the happiness of the people. But the diffusion of an energetic race through distant and uncultivated lands has surely contributed to the permanent welfare of many generations. A rapid growth of the population increases that struggle for existence which appears to be the destiny of mankind.

In taking, however, a more comprehensive view of the history of the world, it must be admitted that from this struggle new nationalities have arisen, whilst the language and the civilization of the mother country have been carried to the furthest regions of the earth.

Mill's philosophy is defective from its

narrowness; and the word liberty is obscured rather than elucidated by his treatise.

Mill's notion of liberty comprises a severe limitation of human freedom, or, as he calls it, the enforcement of restraints upon the conduct of mankind.

Having failed to obtain a satisfactory explanation of the meaning of the word liberty from Mill, the political philosopher and logician, let us try a modern historian.

In his " History of Ireland," Mr. Froude thus writes :—

" There is no word in human language which so charms the ear as liberty ; there is no word which so little pains have been taken to define, or which is used to express ideas more opposite."

When so able a writer as Mr. Froude made this observation, the reader, not unreasonably, hopes that the historian will proceed to explain the meaning of this complex and ambiguous word liberty. The historian thus proceeds :—

" Who is free ? asked the ancient sage ; and he answered his own question, the wise man who is master of himself. Who is free ? asks the modern liberal politician ; and he answers, the man who has a voice in making the laws which he is expected to obey."

Mr. Froude having cited these ancient and modern definitions of liberty, easily disposes of them as insufficient and valueless. He then offers his own explanation in the following words :—" That nation is most free where the laws, by whomsoever framed, correspond most nearly to the will of the Maker of the Universe, by whom, and not by human suffrage, the code of rules is laid down for our obedience. That nation is most a slave which has ceased to believe that such divinely appointed laws exist, and will only be bound by acts which it places on the statute-book."

Here the reader finds an entirely different explanation of liberty. The laws of a free nation must, it is said, correspond to " the will of the Maker of the Universe." Where are men to find this will ? A large portion of the civilized world believes that this divine will is only to be found in the decisions of the Church of Rome. Another portion denies this proposition, and holds that the Church of Rome would impose slavery rather than liberty on the world.

If the word liberty is to remain unexplained until mankind are agreed as to "the will of the Maker of the Universe," we must abandon in despair all hope of a satisfactory elucidation of the most exciting word in the political vocabulary.

Having vainly endeavoured to discover the meaning of the word liberty in the treatise of the logician, and in the eloquent pages of the historian, we may turn as a last resource to the writings of a legal essayist.

In essays on " Liberty, Equality, and Fraternity, by Fitzjames Stephen," the meaning of civil liberty is discussed as follows :—

" All government is a system of restraint and compulsion; preventing men from doing some things and obliging them to do other things. To lay down any universal rules for civil liberty is impracticable. The rules must vary according to the conditions of the community to which they are applied. Men are born members of some society—either so rude that it is called savage, or in a condition more or less civilized. Wherever born, they are not born free. If they survive their childhood—a period of helpless subservience—they find themselves subject to the customs or laws which prevail around them. All the institutions of society are limitations of liberty. How best to reconcile the liberty of individuals with the general interests of society is the problem to be solved.

" Men are not agreed upon the laws which are to form the basis of human society. The laws of marriage are a restriction of liberty, in regard to which men are not agreed. The laws of property are matters of dispute," &c., &c. :

This able writer demolishes natural liberty altogether, and contends that the expression " civil liberty" has not any precise meaning.

The familiar phrases, religious liberty, liberty of the press, liberty of bequest, &c., are only expressions for degrees of freedom qualified by some restrictions in every civilized community.

After reference to the writings of Locke, of John Stuart Mill, of Mr. Froude, and of Sir James Stephen, the result arrived at is, that the phrase natural liberty has no intelligible meaning; civil liberty cannot be defined, as the expression is vague and variable; and personal liberty, " Potestas vivendi ut velis," is not granted to man living under any form of government.

Tocqueville, after contemplating American society, remarked : " Il n'y a rien de moins in-dépendant qu'un citoyen libre."

Democracy has not been favourable to human freedom. The ancient republics imposed a system of drill and discipline incompatible with personal liberty, and they did not even tolerate freedom of opinion.

Political philosophers from Plato to Comte paid little respect to human liberty whenever it interfered with their own theories of government.

The principles enunciated by Plato would warrant the condemnation of Socrates. Comte, as J. Stuart Mill observed, proposed a system of government quite as oppressive and intolerant as any propounded by the ancient philosophers of Greece ;—and in a preceding page it has been shown that Mill suggested man should not " be fruitful, and multiply, and replenish the earth ;" declaring, moreover, that this prohibition of the universal instinct of humanity was not a restriction of human liberty! A Zulu king is not more arbitrary and despotic than a Radical philosopher.

CHAPTER XIII.

OF ARISTOCRACY.

"Vocantur illi optimates quasi optimi."—Cicero.

Aristocracy, according to the meaning of the word, is a form of government where the chief authority is vested in the most eminent men.

The word did not originally signify a class of hereditary rulers, but rather a privileged order to which men might rise by meritorious public service. Aristocracy is now commonly used to designate persons who have inherited social rank not necessarily connected with political power.

Aristocrat is a word of modern origin; it is not in Johnson's Dictionary, but was probably imported from France at the end of the last century. The separation of classes in that country led to the use of appellations, for which in English we have no equivalent terms: "roturier," "vilain," "bourgeois," were designations by which the French nobility stigmatized all other classes of the community. These classes retorted by identifying " aristocrat" with enmity to the people.

Offensive appellations produce more ill-will than graver injuries, as history and daily experience abundantly prove. Hatred, moreover, seems to linger in the breast of a people long after the actual grievance which engendered it has been removed.

According to the strict meaning of the word, the French nobility in the last century were not an aristocracy; they were not the governing class. At an earlier period Lewis XIV did not select his ministers from the nobility; even in the provinces, although he allowed a nobleman to represent the dignity of government, he sent an official "intendant" to administer the affairs.

Political animosity and social jealousy have so deeply discoloured the history of France, that it is difficult, even with the aid of modern writers such as Barante, Tocqueville, Taine, and others, to ascertain the whole truth respecting the French nobility in the last century. It seems that, with the exception of nobles who were of Royal blood, the great mass of the nobility had been deprived of political power, but had been allowed to retain and even to augment the numerous privileges attaching to their rank. The solid fabric of feudalism was gone, but the scaffolding was thus left standing with all its invidious seigniorial and manorial rights, such as tolls on fairs and markets, on roads and bridges, on everything that was moved by land or by water. The trade of the district, the labour of the peasantry, the produce of the soil, were all subject to claims inherited from feudal ages. The nobles, moreover, had contrived to obtain immunities and exemptions from taxation, which pressed consequently with additional weight on the other classes of the community.

The French nobility were a distinct class, an hereditary caste, and inasmuch as all their descendants were noble, and enjoyed the privileges and immunities attaching to their birth, the number of this privileged order became an intolerable burden to the country. Taine, in his book ("L'Ancien Régime") reckons the number of persons of noble blood at the outbreak of the Revolution in 1789 to have amounted to between 130,000 and 140,000. This number is almost incredible, even assuming it to include those who had been allowed by royal favour to purchase titles of nobility, and also persons whose service under the Crown invested them with similar immunities.

High rank in the Army and lucrative appointments in the Church were reserved for persons of noble birth ; and as all promotion, military and ecclesiastical, depended on the pleasure of the sovereign, assiduous attendance at Court was indispensable alike for the ambitious who desired active service, and for the indolent who wished for honours or sinecures. This habit of life in the Court or Camp tended still further to separate the nobility from their countrymen, upon whom they looked down with the pride of privileged rank, and with the arrogance which too often attaches to military command.

Although the French nobility were invested with all these privileges and immunities, such was their mode of life and their contemptuous disregard of economy and of business, that the great majority of the nobles were poor, and many were reduced to absolute indigence

The subdivision of land in France and the peasant proprietary are often ascribed to the Revolution of 1789. This notion appears to be incorrect. The territories belonging to the royal family, to ecclesiastical dignitaries, and corporations were immense, a few nobles had also princely domains ; but throughout France the peasantry were to a great extent the owners of the soil. This ownership of land could be traced back for several centuries.

Arthur Young, who visited France before the Revolution, noticed the large number of land-owners who were in the condition of peasants. Turgot and Necker, when considering the distress of the French peasantry, expressed an opinion that the separate plots of land from frequent subdivision were insufficient to support a family. The ownership of land was not profitable, because the taxes of the state, and the innumerable dues payable on account of old feudal rights, absorbed the produce. The cultivation of the soil was discouraged ; and the land was left barren, while the peasants were starving.

Thus the sense of injustice festering for years in the hearts of the people ;

" Wrongs unredressed or insults unavenged"

stimulated the hatred of a privileged class,

and of hereditary rank. (Hence it is that in France, "Immortale odium et nunquam sanabile vulnus ardet adhuc"). Where inequality had produced so much suffering and offence, equality became the savage outcry of a maddened people, and Rousseau's language was hailed as the gospel of a regenerated nation.

In England the position of the nobility was altogether different.

The English barons in old feudal times constituted a powerful aristocracy. When, however, they determined to resist the demands of the king, they invoked the aid of the collective freemen, and the Great Charter established the rights of the vassals against the barons, as well as the rights of the barons against the sovereign. During the civil wars, called the Wars of the Roses, the old feudal nobility lost their lives and their possessions. Their number had been so far diminished that in the first Parliament of Henry VII only twenty-nine temporal peers received writs of summons. The extinction of the aristocracy facilitated the domination of the Tudors. The laws and liberties of the nation were set aside at the pleasure of the sovereign, and the freedom of the people was only re-established by a rebellion and a revolution.

During the intermediate period the English nobility had little political power; their feudal authority had ceased, their parliamentary influence had not yet arisen. Nothing of feudalism was in fact left, except some legal forms and fictions, which lawyers derived, or pretended to derive, from Norman or Saxon antiquity.

The English nobility did not constitute a separate class of society. Commoners were raised to the peerage, and the sons of peers become commoners. The nobility had no exemptions from taxation, and their political influence depended on their wealth, their abilities, or their character.

Thus the nobility subsided into country gentlemen and lived as equals amongst their neighbours. A new source of political power was now open to them, and their sons or relations became the accepted representatives of the people in Parliament.

It is often asserted, especially by foreign historians, that the Revolution of 1688 was accomplished by the English aristocracy. The leading statesmen of that period were not the hereditary descendants of a feudal nobility; they possessed no territorial power. Danby, Nottingham, Halifax, Shaftesbury, and Marlborough were new peers, who had risen from the commonalty by their abilities, and were supported by a large portion of the educated classes, and by the Churchmen and Dissenters, who were alarmed for the Protestant religion.

During the eighteenth century the peers, in common with other landowners, acquired great influence in the House of Commons, but until towards the end of the century no popular discontent appears to have been occasioned on this account. Burke, in the year 1770, writing "On the Cause of the Present Discontents, did not allude to the necessity of Parliamentary reform or to the state of the representation in the House of Commons. If the influence of the peers had been a general ground of dissatisfaction, he could hardly have avoided all reference to it. An extensive change in the distribution of the people had not yet occurred. The steam-engine was in truth one of the motive powers which produced the Reform Bill; although as early as 1780 an amendment of the representation had been advocated in Parliament, and might then have been most advantageously adopted.

It has been said that in some former age the English peasantry were landed proprietors, that " they tilled the land, but owned the land they tilled." The artisan also in former times " worked the loom, but owned the loom he worked."

A workman who has no capital is forced, when a crop fails or trade languishes, to mortgage his land or to pawn his loom. The report on the hand-loom weavers proved the futility of attempting to maintain an industrial occupation which had been superseded by a more economical system of manufacture. So also in husbandry; agriculture on a larger scale was found to be more profitable: the steam-plough superseded the spade, machinery was introduced, and the capitalist throve, where the poorer peasant failed.

Any person acquainted with the Western counties will admit that, when a property consists of a few acres, it is almost invariably mortgaged to the banker or solicitor in the neighbouring town.

Lifehold and copyhold tenures were common in a former century, but were notoriously unfavourable to improvement, and have been wisely abandoned.

Many social and political problems are

involved in the tenure of land, which have never been sufficiently examined.

In Bancroft's "History of the United States" it is said that the first emigrants from England began with a scheme of common property in land. This system, however, occasioned such discontent that it was speedily abandoned. Another scheme was next tried; parcels of land were assigned for cultivation, but not for inheritance. This scheme was also found unsatisfactory, and the emigrants were compelled to revert to the system of the Old World, and to allot the land in perpetual fee.

The compulsory sub-division of landed property in France has produced results unfavourable to the increase of the population. Thus it is observed that, while the British race and the English language are spreading over a large portion of the globe, the French people scarcely increase in number, and the French language will soon be restricted to the French soil.

This check to the population produces for a

10 *

limited number of persons a more comfortable livelihood; but for the greatest happiness of the greatest number, we may point to thriving communities in Canada, in Australia, and in New Zealand.

A considerable change is, however, perceptible in this country among the owners of land. The smaller proprietors are leaving their old abodes, and emigrating to towns or to the Continent. Land is so burdened with rates and taxes, that it is an undesirable investment. The opportunities for educating children and the attractions of society induce persons to abandon the rural life of a former century; whilst sale of their land enables them to employ their money to greater advantage. This change is to be regretted, because it has deprived the counties of a class of men who were useful for the administration of local affairs.

In every civilized country there will arise a class of men who having inherited wealth are released from the necessity of manual labour

and from the drudgery of professional employment. Even under Republican institutions,
this class will gradually assume many of the
characteristics of a social aristocracy. They
attach importance to inherited names, to family
connections, and they like to trace out an
ancestral history.

They cultivate refinement in their tastes and
studies. They associate with the educated
society of other countries, from which they
acquire enlarged views and varied experience.

A form of government which repudiates and
ostracises this class is defective. It loses the
benefit of abilities which run to waste, and
drives men, who are not unfit for public
employment, to pass their lives in enforced
idleness at home, or to seek for congenial
society abroad.

Political affairs meanwhile, being entirely
relinquished to the industrial classes, and to
men who hope to derive a livelihood from
office, are lowered to a trade, and pur-

sued in a sordid spirit as a profitable employment.

The Americans are in their hearts an aristocratic people, living under democratic institutions. This sentiment frequently peeps out from under the domino which the Republic forces them to wear.

ENTAILS.

Adam Smith, alluding to the law of entail at that period, said, " Nothing can be more completely absurd, than that the property of the present generation should be regulated according to the fancy of those who died perhaps five hundred years ago." He contended that the property of great land-owners was always worse managed than the estates of small proprietors.

This statement could not now be maintained with truth. The law of entail has also been restricted since the time of Adam Smith.

It may be doubted, however, whether the law

of entail as modified by later statutes is beneficial to peers or to the landed gentry. The law renders the possessor of land dependent on the next heir. In many cases this is an impediment to improvements. A worse result is, that it enables a youth, possessed of strong passions and little self-control, to sell his reversion to money-lenders. The actual possessor then finds himself displaced, and is compelled either to buy back his estate or to look forward to its ruin.

The subject is, however, involved in some difficulty, and would require to be carefully considered in connection with the law and custom of settlements in cases of marriage.

The abolition of the power of entail would probably disappoint the Democratic party, who wish to subdivide estates, to extinguish the large landowners, to pull down " the pinnacles of Burghley and the oriels of Longleat," for the purpose of planting cabbage gardens.

In this country there is a strong feeling in favour of hereditary dignities. Men highly value honours and distinctions which they can bequeath to their children; they wish to see their name preserved to future ages, and associated with a property in some district where their parents lived, or in which their early years were passed. This sentiment is an incentive to exertion which it seems unwise in statesmen altogether to despise and reject.

Adam Smith regarded lineal succession and the custom of primogeniture as foolish superstitions; but they are deeply seated in the hearts of men, and have induced them

" To scorn delights and live laborious days "

in order that their descendants may look back with pride and emulation to an ancestor who has won a place of honour in his country's history.

" Non omnis moriar, multaque pars mei
Vitabit Libitinam."

This impulse inspired a Roman poet, and in some form it is common to the human race, although it is the germ of that sentiment which is hateful to democracy. The opposite sentiment of equality is indeed more fully gratified when generation after generation passes to the grave, undistinguished and unremembered, in one uniform level of insignificance.

CHAPTER XIV.

ENVY THE ANIMATING SPIRIT OF DEMOCRACY.

"Il ne faut pas se dissimuler que les institutions démocratiques développent à un très haut degré le sentiment de l'envie dans le cœur humain."—TOCQUEVILLE.

THE French revolution of 1789, in vindictive hatred of the gross injustice of " l'ancien régime," rushed into the opposite extreme, and denounced all superiority of rank, of authority, of wealth, and of genius. When the revolutionary tribunal condemned to death Lavoisier, the most distinguished chemist in Europe, the judge accompanied the sentence with this emphatic declaration, " Nous n'avons plus besoin de savants."

The same sentiment may be traced in the later writings of the French Socialists. They permitted in their scheme of society, literature, science, and art to be studied, stipulating that the study should not confer distinction.

" Sera artiste qui voudra, à la condition de redevenir laboureur, et de laisser le pinceau ou le ciseau pour retourner à la charrue."

According to the same principle of levelling all inequalities, they condemned property as a pregnant source of injustice.

"Celui qui osera prononcer le mot propriété sera enfermé comme fou furieux."

If perfect social equality is the object to be attained, the language of the French Socialists is logical. Property, learning, genius, muscular strength, tend to inequality of conditions. The difficulty consists in the application of the principle of equality. If all men were reduced to absolute poverty and compelled to live as troglodytes in caves or hollow trees, some would still complain that one cave was damp while another was dry, and the principle of equality was violated.

In this country the revolutionary doctrine of

equality has not been formulated as the basis of social life, but it is a tenet cherished by working men. One man must not earn more wages than his fellows, do better work, or acquire any superiority inconsistent with equality of profit. To this extent personal liberty is restricted, improvement checked, and progress discountenanced.

An analogous sentiment seems to animate some men against the Established Church. They cannot complain that the Church injures them ; but they envy the social position of the clergy, and the honours of the Episcopate. They wish to

> " See no contiguous palace rear its head,
> To shame the meanness of their humble shed."

The uneducated labourer does not require a learned clergy ; and the greatest happiness of the greatest number would be better served by the preaching of some " Jeremiah Ringletub " than by the most refined scholarship which Cambridge or Oxford could produce.

Rousseau's notion that equality is the ordinance of nature displays the wild predominance of his imagination. Nature knows nothing of equality. Her products are never equal. No certain measure of length or of capacity can be found in nature. Variety and inequality are universal in the animal and vegetable creation. What nature indicates, human society requires, or anarchy would reign supreme; as Shakespeare truly said :—

> " Take but degree away, untune that string
> And hark, what discord follows."

CHAPTER XV.

LORD MACAULAY states in his history that
before the Revolution of 1688, although there
were ministers of the Crown, they did not constitute what we call a ministry; that is, a small
body of men who, supported by a majority in
Parliament, are agreed upon the general policy to
be pursued in the management of public affairs.

This scheme was, he says, first adopted in
the reign of William and Mary. The ministry
was not for many years so compact a body as
Macaulay's language would indicate. In the
early part of the eighteenth century ministers
openly opposed one another: and it was only
by degrees that unity of political opinion became so far the attribute of Cabinet ministers,

that they assumed a joint responsibility for their policy and public measures.

Macaulay praises the institution of a Cabinet as a contrivance of consummate wisdom, inasmuch as it secured to Parliament a paramount influence over the executive government, without depriving the government of the proper functions of administration.

Without intending to depreciate this political contrivance, which is a necessity in our Parliamentary system, it must be admitted that the institution of the Cabinet has tended to diminish the personal responsibility of each individual minister, and to intensify party government by generating a combined opposition.

The responsibility of each minister is now sheltered behind the screen of the Cabinet. If the official conduct of a minister becomes the subject of animadversion in Parliament, the united Cabinet defend their colleague and claim to share his responsibility. The whole political party then rush to the rescue of the government, and although in private they may blame the minister as a blunderer or jobber, in public they absolve him from all censure, and even lavish eulogies on his many virtues.

The responsibility of the Cabinet can only be enforced by a Parliamentary vote. In this case the judges are not impartial, inasmuch as both sides have a direct interest in the decision; one party desire to retain the ministry in office, the other party desire to occupy their places. The country therefore rightly regards a vote of censure, not as an honest judgment, but as a party victory.

Burke noticed with regret that the responsibility of ministers was much diminished. "The House of Commons," he said, "sitting for a great part of the year, has gradually approximated to the character of a standing senate, and has thus lost its control, because it is made to partake in every considerable act of the government."

Burke, moreover, deplored that "impeachment, that great guardian of the purity of the Constitution, is in danger of being lost even to the idea of it."

This loss will not be regretted by any modern politician. The power of impeachment was much misused. The Earl of Oxford was impeached for concluding the Peace of Utrecht. But this was a flagrant act of injustice and of party spite; inasmuch as a previous House of Commons had pronounced the peace to be beneficial. The impeachment of Warren Hastings, although it afforded an opportunity for brilliant oratory, was discreditable to the Commons, who in after years endeavoured to make some amends for this lengthened persecution of an able public servant.

The institution of a Cabinet with joint responsibility renders it difficult to condemn any individual minister for a public measure; and the most vindictive politician would hardly propose to send the whole Cabinet to the Tower. In modern times, indeed, politicians have found the Tower to be, not the dreary dungeon of the condemned statesman, but the gateway to popularity and fame.

In the year 1854 Baron Stockmar wrote what Mr. Theodore Martin calls " a vigorous constitutional essay " for the instruction of the Prince Consort.

Baron Stockmar states in this treatise that " the old Tories, who, before the Reform Bill, were in power for fifty years, had a direct interest in upholding the prerogatives of the Crown, and they did uphold them manfully, although the Hanoverian kings, by their immoral, politically exceptionable, dynastic or private wishes and interests, made the task anything but an easy one."

" As a race," Baron Stockmar adds, " these Tories have died out, and the race, which in the present day bears their name, are simply degenerate bastards. Our Whigs, again, are nothing but partly conscious, partly unconscious Republicans, who stand in the same relation to the throne as the wolf does to the lamb." . . . If the English Crown permit a Whig ministry to follow their opinions in practice, "you must not wonder, if in a little time you find the majority of the people mpressed with the belief, that the king, in the view of the law, is nothing but a mandarin figure, which has to nod its head in assent, or shake it in denial, as his minister pleases."

Baron Stockmar, having thus disposed of the Tories and of the Whigs, says of the Aberdeen School that "they treat the existing Constitution merely as a bridge to a Republic."

The opinion of the German Baron would be unworthy of notice, except for his acknowledged influence in the highest quarter. It is, however, painful to read the reply of the Prince Consort, who, being intimately acquainted with these statesmen, writes to the Baron:—"I heartily agree with every word you say."

The imputation of disloyalty and hypocrisy

cast against the leaders of all parties was un-
deserved, and proves the Baron to have been a
prejudiced counsellor. Fortunately, the Prince
Consort was not guided in his public conduct
by the whimsical notions of Baron Stockmar.

It must be admitted that under the British
Constitution the Prime Minister is the head
of a political party. He may be a politician
of no official experience, having acquired his
position by skill in debate, or by his adroitness
in guiding his followers. When in office, his
time is chiefly occupied in defending his position against ambitious opponents, and in conciliating dissatisfied adherents. Thus, abilities
which should be devoted to the service of the
state, are often employed in schemes for
strengthening his majority or defeating the
attack of his assailants.

Every form of government, however, has its
inherent defects; and under an absolute
monarch the intrigues of a court are as
pernicious and debasing as the manœuvres

resorted to for manipulating a representative assembly.

A representative government is disadvantageously situated in treating with foreign powers. An absolute sovereign usually selects for the management of foreign affairs a man who has been trained in office, and who is experienced in all the complex history and antecedents of European diplomacy. The minister selected, having the confidence of his royal master, can give his undivided attention to the business of his department and to the interests of his country.

The British minister is chosen for the convenience of party arrangements, and must learn the details of foreign affairs after his appointment, or rely upon the permanent officers of the department. He knows that, whatever his policy may be, it will be attacked, and, so far as possible, thwarted in Parliament. Foreign Governments will be told that his measures are disapproved by the British people, and, consequently, his authority is weakened, and his assurances received with distrust. It will often, moreover, be perceived that his despatches are written, not for the Government to which they are addressed, but for re-production in the British Parliament.

Public life in this country may fit a member of Parliament indifferently-well for any other office, but seldom qualifies him to represent his country adequately among the practised diplomatists of foreign states.

The enthusiastic believers in European progress maintained that the force of public opinion and the influence of democracy would tend to create more amicable relations among states, and to promote international confidence, increased commerce, and a general desire for peace.

Lamartine, in the " Histoire des Girondins," affirmed that one of the sublime, almost divine truths which the French Revolution of 1789 had established in politics was, " La souve-

raineté du droit sur la force." This was a
startling statement to make after the empire
of the first Napoleon.   Not, however, to revert
to that period, let us see what public opinion
has effected in recent years.

The treatment of Denmark by Prussia and
Austria was correctly described by M. Drouyn
de Lhuys, when he wrote in reference to these
spoliations, " Nous regrettons de n'y trouver
d'autre fondement que la force."

From that date the supremacy of force has
been insolently avowed as a sufficient justification for the armed interference of the great
military powers; and the public opinion of
states which profess to be democratic, such as
Italy, is quite as aggressive as the absolute
sovereigns of the north.

It appears, therefore, that democracy affords
in itself no guarantee for European peace.

THE COUNCIL—LUCUS A NON LUCENDO.

The newspapers inform us that on some

previous day the sovereign held a council, and it might be supposed according to the usual meaning of the word, that a council is an assembly of persons met together for consultation. Such councils were held in former centuries, and were sanctioned by the royal presence. The king often took an active part in the proceedings, rebuking the members and controlling the decisions. Of such councils the reign of Queen Anne supplies the last example.

In modern times the council is a meeting where the sovereign is present, but where no consultation takes place. The council is now a court formality, useful for the solemn announcement and publication of measures and appointments previously sanctioned by the king, but not in any sense an assembly for deliberation.

The Cabinet meanwhile has appropriated the deliberative functions which belonged in ancient times to the council board.

THE CABINET.

The chief executive powers of the state are vested in the Cabinet, which is a committee of members of Parliament, holding the highest administrative offices and meeting to consult upon measures to be submitted, first for the approval of the sovereign, and subsequently for the decision of Parliament.

This body is in a somewhat anomalous position; it is unrecognized by the laws, it keeps no record of its meetings or of its proceedings, and it exists only by an honourable understanding between the members. Since no record of differences, of discussions, or of arguments is kept, it is a point of honour not to refer to conversations which cannot afterwards be authenticated. All the members of the Cabinet are collectively responsible for the decisions arrived at, and if any member differs from his colleagues, he must determine for himself whether he will acquiesce and share the responsibility, or quit the Cabinet and resign his office. Even after his resignation, he should be scrupulously careful not to reveal what has occurred in the Cabinet, further than is indispensable for his own justification; and even for this partial revelation he must ask the permission of the sovereign. A subsequent reference to conversations in the Cabinet is worthless, unless the matter has been recorded in a letter, and accepted as a correct statement of the divergent opinions.

On one occasion the Constitutional position of the Cabinet was matter of discussion in Parliament. In the year 1806, during the Grenville Ministry, Lord Ellenborough, who was then Chief Justice, was made a Cabinet Minister. The appointment of the highest criminal judge to be a member of the executive government was noticed in Parliament as irregular and objectionable. The discussion, however, terminated by a general admission in both Houses that the Cabinet has no organized or corporate character, and is altogether unrecognized by the Constitution.

It seems an anomaly that the chief executive power of the state should be vested in a body which is altogether unrecognized by law, and unacknowledged by the Constitution.

Where nothing is fixed by law, the engagement of honour becomes the more imperative. Every minister is thus bound to his colleagues to keep them informed of every important departmental proceeding, so that the Cabinet may not be committed to a policy without its deliberate approval.

Every minister is equally bound in honour and loyalty to his sovereign not to do any act which may by implication convey the royal assent, unless the matter has been previously explained to the king, and has received the royal sanction.

These honourable engagements have not always been scrupulously observed.

OPEN QUESTIONS.

The institution of a ministry has been already declared to be a political contrivance indispensable for the management of public affairs under a Parliamentary government. There have, however, been ministries wherein the members have held office together without a cordial agreement upon questions of great national importance, and in such cases the expedient of what are called open questions has been adopted.

This contrivance appears to have been first introduced as an avowed system by Lord Liverpool in the year 1812, with reference to the Roman Catholic claims. Lord Castlereagh explained this novel principle to the House of Commons in these words:—

" In submission to the growing change of public opinion in favour of these claims, and the sentiments of certain members of the Government, it has been resolved upon as a principle that the discussion of this question should be left free from all interference on the part of the Government, and that every member of that Government should on it be left to the free and unbiassed suggestions of his own conscientious discretion."

Lord Liverpool, in thus leaving every member of the Government free to exercise his own judgment on the most important question of domestic policy, abdicated the first duty of a minister, and established a most pernicious precedent, without any justification. So long as George III could attend to affairs of state, his strong religious feeling and the diseased condition of his intellect, afforded an excuse for not proposing a measure to which he conscientiously objected. But in the year 1812, the King's recovery was known to be hopeless, and the Catholic question might have been advantageously settled. During that session it was carried by a large majority (a majority of two to one) in the House of

Commons, and only rejected by one vote in the House of Lords.

An unworthy compliance with the capricious objection of the Regent (who had himself indulged in a mock marriage with a Roman Catholic), left this irritating question for seventeen years festering in the breasts of the Irish people, many of whom were then loyally fighting side by side with Protestant soldiers under the command of Wellington.

Although this contrivance of open questions was introduced by a Tory Ministry for the gratification of royalty, it has been since more frequently resorted to by the opposite party.

A ministry which avows itself to be neutral, and to have no fixed opinion on an important public matter, is in a discreditable position. This course of proceeding has been adopted to facilitate the united action of irreconcilable partisans; or else to obtain office under the mask of moderation, which mask is to be thrown aside whenever a convenient opportunity is offered.

Open questions are found convenient for the purpose of conciliating provincial politicians, —that class of narrow-minded electors, who attach more importance to some special measure, such as liberty to marry a deceased wife's sister, than to the general interests of the nation.

Candidates are induced to humour these whimsical voters by accepting pledges on such matters, in boroughs, where political parties are nearly balanced ; and the result of these contests is afterwards trumpeted as a glorious party victory.

Such pledges have an immoral tendency, encouraging reckless politicians, and repelling respectable and conscientious candidates.

This effect of popular representation is, however, intimately connected with a more important problem, namely, the influence of different forms of government on the moral character of a people.

Political morality is in this country below

the general moral tone of educated society; and inasmuch as the extension of the franchise will include a lower class of voters, it must be expected that political morality will deteriorate rather than improve.

Absolute government and unrestricted democracy are both unfavourable to the character of a nation; but under every form of government the inducements to discreditable practices are so numerous, that political writers seem to regard the moral amelioration of a community to be no part of the duty of government.

CHAPTER XVI.

OF PROGRESS.

A BELIEF that mankind are advancing in knowledge, in virtue, and in happiness, would be a gratifying prospect of the future destiny of the human race. If we felt confident that the influence of democracy would accelerate this desirable result, who would not be a democrat ?

So far, however, as our limited experience enables us to judge of the effects of democratic rule, it appears to be ill-adapted to develop the higher qualities of mankind. Man's nature is compounded of such a variety of heterogeneous elements, that the preponderating power of any one class of men, although it may be the most numerous class, will operate unfavourably on

12

that complex organization of society which we now call civilized.

What, then, is the meaning which we attach to the word Civilization? The term in the sense in which it is now used is of recent origin. In Johnson's Dictionary the word is only said to denote the commutation of a criminal into a civil process. The French Academy did not admit the word in their dictionary until Guizot had delivered his celebrated lectures on Civilization, after the defeat and overthrow of the first Napoleon.

In his opening lecture, Guizot said that progress was inseparably connected with the idea of civilization. John Stuart Mill, more correctly, observed that the word is used in two senses: in an active sense, signifying the process of civilizing or being civilized; and in a passive sense, denoting the state of advancement to which any society may have attained.

In almost every condition of human life some rudiments of civilization may be perceived.

The pre-historic man who sharpened broken flints and polished implements of bone was not altogether uncivilized.

The notion of progress seems to be a modern idea. Among the ancient nations any change was more dreaded than desired. The wisest of Hebrew monarchs said that the future would resemble the past: "the thing that has been is that which shall be," &c., &c. The earliest poets believed that the human race was deteriorating. The philosophers taught that the world revolved in cycles, and that any great amelioration of man's condition was a vain dream.

In the material world, the animal and vegetable productions displayed no signs of progress. An uniform and monotonous rotation seemed to be the course ordained in the heaven above as in the earth beneath, and there was no proof that man was exempted from the scheme of the visible universe. History justified this gloomy view of human destiny.

12 *

Nations which attained great power had again perished, they had left ruined walls and tombs as the only record of their existence.

Buckle, in his interesting but unfinished history, inquired whether civilization had been most promoted by the cultivation of man's intellectual or of his moral qualities; and he pronounced in favour of the intellectual. Thus he considered the Athenians had attained a higher civilization than the Romans. The Athenians were superior in art and literature. The Romans were pre-eminent in military organization, in jurisprudence, and in government. The characteristics of the Roman mind —fortitude, perseverance, fidelity to engagements—were, however, qualities more conducive to national greatness than the artistic skill and literary excellence of the Athenians; although these last have probably gained the higher admiration of posterity.

Modern civilization has inherited or acquired something from every preceding generation:

from the East, religion; from Greece, arts and literature; from Rome, municipal institutions and jurisprudence. Even from the feudal ages some noble qualities have descended to us— energetic self-reliance, loyalty, and that chivalrous feeling, the mixture of pride and self-respect, which, in the absence of higher motives, often controlled the actions of the powerful, and pleaded in behalf of those who were weak and helpless.

It would not be easy to apportion, justly, to bygone ages the share which is due to each in these various bequests. The traditional celebrity and exquisite beauty of Grecian literature have induced modern authors to ascribe to Greece in philosophy and politics more than civilization really owes to that over-praised race.

The influence of the Greek mind tended to retard science, to misguide politics, and to corrupt religion.

First, as to progress in science. The Greek

philosophers were deficient in the faculty of
pursuing knowledge by observation and ex-
periment. They found it more agreeable to
frame new theories than patiently to collect
facts and trace their sequence and connexion.
Thus in physical science they made no advance :
studying words and definitions rather than the
visible objects around them, they became the
slaves of their own language, and rejected the
outside world. Socrates, a man whose intellectual capacity might have imparted new
vigour to the Athenian mind, instead of guiding
his countrymen towards the study of nature,
denounced such pursuits, and argued that "the
Gods intended the machinery by which they
brought about astronomical and physical results
to remain unknown, and that it was impious as
well as useless to pry into such secrets."

The consequence was that the schools of
Greek philosophy, instead of expanding and
fertilizing the minds of later generations,
cramped and confined the human intellect,

until the pedants and drivellers of the Byzantine Empire brought philosophy and learning into contempt.

In politics the Greeks confined their views to their own limited horizon. A thoughtful politician must be astonished at the blindness of Aristotle. A man, who had lived at the court of Philip and witnessed the disciplined strength of Macedonia, nevertheless persists in propounding, as the best form of government, a republic so small that it would be perfectly helpless. This, moreover, at an epoch when, whatever forms of government might thereafter be established, these miniature republics, or rather oligarchies, based on slavery, were about to disappear for ever from the face of the earth.

The Greek mind exercised a most pernicious influence on Christianity, by attempting to define and subdivide the nature of the Deity, and disputing over incomprehensible mysteries. The civilized world still suffers from these verba subtleties and unintelligible definitions. Many centuries have elapsed since Greece spoke her last word in literature, in politics, and in religion. Three hundred years before the Christian era, her mental vigour was declining; and Grote, her most enthusiastic historian, closes his history at that epoch with "feelings of sadness and humiliation."

At a time when the claims of Greece are put forward on account of her ancient services to civilization, this short digression may not be altogether useless.

Modern civilization owes more to Imperial Rome than to Ancient Greece for progress in all matters connected with politics.

Gibbon, however, somewhat overvalued the Roman administration under the Antonines, when he said: "If a man were called upon to fix the period in the history of the world during which the condition of the human race was most happy and prosperous, he would, without hesitation, name that which elapsed from the death of Domitian to the accession of Commodus."

With all respect to this distinguished historian, a man might reasonably hesitate to pronounce any confident opinion on the subject, feeling that the state of the Roman provinces at the period named is insufficiently known. This fact at least must be placed in the opposite scale in weighing the merits of the best imperial government : slavery, with a large trade in slaves, was an established institution, and must have been attended with much human suffering and degradation.

It is apparently true that Imperial Rome at that period maintained the peace and good order of the civilized world with an army of 300,000 men ; and we should now gladly rest and be thankful with such a limited military establishment.

The growth of municipal institutions contributed to civil liberty, to industrial improvement, and to refinement in all the arts, which

usually accompany the accumulation of wealth.
For these advantages Europe was indebted to
Ancient Rome.

After the collapse of the Roman Empire, the
Italian republics, emanating from the organization of municipal institutions, seemed for a
time to afford some security for freedom and
for political progress. These republics, however, sank under the overwhelming violence
of democracy. As Guizot observes, " La
liberté y était si orageuse, si redoutable, que
les hommes la prenaient bientôt, si non en
dégôut, du moins en terreur, et cherchaient à
tout prix un ordre politique qui leur donnât
quelque securité, but essentiel et condition
absolue de l'état social."

The Italian people relinquished their national
independence, and submitted to a foreign
domination, in order to escape from the tyranny
of an ignorant and turbulent multitude.

Freedom, however, in a rude fashion, still
survived in the North of Europe, and was

gradually consolidated in this country under a system of representation. In former chapters the practical working of this system has been discussed ; so far at least as to indicate an opinion that this political institution cannot be the last stage in the political progress of the civilized world.

By what means its glaring imperfections are to be remedied, or by what system of government it may eventually be superseded, must be decided by the dispassionate judgment of future generations. It may be sufficient here to state, that this boasted institution, judged by its moral, or rather its immoral, effect on the character of the nation, is a blot on our civilization.

The noble science of government has degenerated into the ignoble art of electioneering, with all its debasing concomitants.

To express an opinion on political and moral progress without any reference to the influence of religious thought, may appear to be an unjustifiable omission. This subject, however, belongs to an entirely different mental condition. The sacred seed was planted in the human mind, and left to grow in purity and in strength. In regard to the religious progress of the future, this statement may nevertheless be cited as deserving the consideration of thoughtful politicians. " Toute forme positive, quelque satisfaisante qu'elle soit pour le présent, contient un germe d'opposition au progrès de l'avenir."

The past history of the world in every civilized country seems to confirm the truth of this observation.

We often flatter ourselves that the progress of Great Britain is owing to the qualities of the British race, to their indomitable energy, to their love of freedom, to their obedience to law, and to the innumerable other virtues with which we readily credit ourselves. This opinion is not perhaps altogether accurate, if we allow it to be examined more closely.

The progress of a nation—that is, its advance in population, in knowledge, in wealth, and in power—appears to be influenced by a variety of circumstances, one of which is its geographical position.

Mr. Gladstone, in an essay called " Kin beyond Sea," which he published in the *North American Review* in the autumn of 1878, seems to have neglected this important element of national prosperity.

In this essay he contemplated with philosophic complacency an approaching time when the commercial pre-eminence of this country would be superseded by the United States of North America.

He has, he says, no inclination to murmur at this prospect. He will see trade decline, wealth diminish, industry depressed with all the miseries attendant on national decay, without any discomposure of his serene temperament ;

" Si fractus illabatur orbis
Impavidum ferient ruinæ."

Great Britain is to sink into a subordinate position, or, to use Mr. Gladstone's words, she is " to cease to be the head servant in the great household of the world."

This is not a flattering title for our position in the community of nations ; but even from this humble and menial situation we are to be displaced. The sentence thus pronounced upon us appears the more severe, inasmuch as we, who are now the only adherents of free trade, are to be driven from the markets of the world by a rival nation, which has been nursed and raised to this supremacy under a system of protection.

As Venice and Genoa yielded to other nations the primacy of mercantile greatness and naval power, so also Britannia is, we are told, doomed to let fall the sceptre of the seas, and we ought to prepare for the day of our affliction. It might be expected from Mr. Gladstone's lugubrious language that the long-predicted New Zealander would shortly arrive with his sketch-book in his hand, to secure the last picturesque record of our dilapidated condition.

It may, however, be some consolation to reflect that, without reference to forms of government, the geographical position of Venice, in the altered condition of oceanic commerce, necessarily placed this maritime city at a disadvantage. The same reasoning would apply to Genoa and even to Holland; we may be allowed therefore to take a more cheerful view of the services we may yet perform in " the great household of the world."

There is yet one branch of human progress which we may contemplate with unmixed satisfaction, and that is the progress of science, both in its discoveries and its adaptations to the convenience and civilization of mankind. It may be hoped that the acquisitions of science may become an enduring benefit to the world, not to be again obliterated and lost amid the political convulsions to which society may be subjected.

To this progress the scientific men of every country may contribute, whether they live under a despotism or under a Constitutional government. The pursuit of truth for its own sake is the noblest occupation of the human mind, and from this pursuit it seems probable that mankind will reap the richest reward.

G. NORMAN AND SON, PRINTERS, 29, MAIDEN LANE, COVENT GARDEN.

www.ingramcontent.com/pod-product-compliance
Lightning Source LLC
Chambersburg PA
CBHW030834270326
41928CB00007B/1053